Railway Memories

CLEVELAND

&

WHITBY

Stephen Chapman

Teesside personified. Q6 0-8-0 No. 63343 heads an eastbound 1950s freight past the closed Newport station as the huge mass of engineering that is the Newport bridge looms above it. Newport bridge could raise its road deck to 120ft above high water level enabling large ships to pass underneath, and was the biggest vertical lift bridge in the world when built by local steelmaking giant Dorman Long in 1934. It was raised for the last time in November 1990 and is now permanently fixed. *Neville Stead collection*

BELLCODE BOOKS
21 DALE AVENUE
TODMORDEN
WEST YORKSHIRE OL14 6BA
email: bellcode4books@yahoo.co.uk

Edited by Steve Chapman

Printed by the Amadeus Press Ltd., Cleckheaton, West Yorks.

Practically everything in this relatively recent Battersby scene has gone since this picture was taken in 1989. The signals and the signal box were replaced in the early 1990s by an automated control system, while the Class 143 Pacers were transferred to South Wales around the same time. The water tank, once noted for its resident goldfish, is still there along with the water column which is now minus its bag. *Stephen Chapman*

INTRODUCTION

There's no mistaking the wild splendour of the North Yorkshire Moors, the rugged heights of the Cleveland Hills or the man-made volcanic horizons of Teesside.

The mass concentration of engineering, steel and chemical plants along the south bank of the River Tees stand testimony to the great industrial tradition of Cleveland. Yet, travel just a few miles inland to the unspoilt beauty of the Cleveland Hills and it is almost impossible to imagine that this rural landscape was also a hive of industry when the 19th century saw events akin to a Wild West gold rush.

Although coal was the initial motivation behind Cleveland's first railway and the founding of Middlesbrough itself, it was the dash for iron which brought railways spreading like briars around the inland hills and dales.

Countless branch lines, standard and narrow gauge industrial railways, tramways and inclines probed into the hills in search of the prized ore - urgently needed to make the metal that built industrial Britain, its empire and more railways.

These branches came and went with the ironstone mines they served and with iron mining peaking around the 1870s many of them had gone by the start of the 20th century. But the through routes with their passenger services and other forms of goods traffic made it at least to the 1960s.

In **Railway Memories No.18** we revisit Cleveland's railways as we remember them in the 1950s and 60s - when they still went to such places as Guisborough, Boosbeck and beyond Boulby along the cliff tops to Whitby, when Stokesley was on a through route from Whitby to Stockton and when the area shuddered to the weight of something like 500 goods trains every 24 hours, some of them still bringing ironstone down from the last mines to the furnaces of Teesside.

It may seem odd that the Rosedale railway is mentioned only in passing but it is well documented elsewhere and had closed long before the era covered by the Railway Memories series.

On 7th September 1964 British Railways began using the 24-hour clock in its working timetables so we use am and pm up to that date and thereafter the 24-hour clock except where direct comparisons are made between times of different eras.

Contents

Of Cleveland's inland railways, only the Middlesbrough-Battersby - Whitby route lasted beyond the 1960s.
Although retaining much of its charm, the Esk Valley line doesn't look much like this nowadays. A8 4-6-2T No. 69861 of Whitby shed rolls a Middlesbrough-Whitby train into Kildale station in the early 1950s.
In 2007 a single track uses the platform on the left but the right hand platform, a small building and even the nameboard in the picture survive beneath a covering of ivy. *J. W. Armstrong Trust*

The iron roads of Cleveland

Cleveland occupies the North East corner of Yorkshire - around 250 square miles of diversity situated between the Tees estuary and the Esk Valley which divides the Cleveland Hills from the North Yorkshire Moors. It contains some of Britain's finest countryside, its highest cliffs, three major seaside resorts, a racecourse, various docks and fishing villages, huge steelworks and one of Britain's last big iron smelters, Europe's deepest mine, vast chemical plants and many other industries.

The liasic rocks forming the Cleveland and North Yorkshire uplands rise to over 1000ft above sea level from a line about four miles south of the Tees. In the east they clash with the North Sea, abruptly terminating with cliffs towering to over 670ft. Impure limestone and shale, these rocks were of little commercial value but below them lay beds of oolitic ironstone extending beneath both the Cleveland Hills and the Moors to outcrop on the northern slopes, on the sides of various dales, and in the cliffs. Mining began in quantity during the early 1800s and at first most of the output was shipped away from the area but as the industrial revolution gathered pace, a growing demand for iron on Teesside coupled with newly accessible coking coal and good quality limestone in nearby South West Durham soon led to mass iron making in Cleveland. It has been said that when ironstone mining was at its peak in the mid to late 19th century there were over 60 mines, 50 of them within a seven-mile radius of Guisborough. Some iron works were established near the mines and although they were short-lived, bigger and more efficient plants on the south bank of the Tees have lasted to the present day.

Alum abounded in the cliffs around Whitby and extensive workings which remain visible to this day grew up along the coast in the 17th century. Combined with ammonia(stale urine collected from countless privvies), it was once used for fixing wool dyes. Together with salt deposits in the marshy ground bordering the Tees, it is reputed to have triggered Teesside's great chemical industry.

As in many areas, however, coal was the driving force behind Teesside's first railway. Soon after its 1825 opening, the Stockton & Darlington Railway outgrew its coal shipping quay at Stockton and urgently needed better facilities for handling the ever growing volume of coal its trains were bringing from the pits of South West Durham. Extending its line across the Tees to a point four and a half miles down river, it established coal staithes at a remote spot it named Port Darlington; a passenger terminus was also provided, just west of the custom house. Opened in December 1830, the extension helped shipping by being that much nearer the sea, avoiding a tortuous stretch of river and enabling the use of larger vessels.

With the extension came Middlesbrough - a new town built from scratch and the first in the world to be started as the result of a railway. Seeing rich development potential, a consortium including members of the Pease family who had estates in the area as well as interests in the S&D, bought 520 acres of virgin land immediately east of Port Darlington and there they built Middlesbrough - an area later known as Old Town. The town spread inland and became a classic example of the 19th Century 'grid iron' street layout. In a 1920s pamphlet for the London & North Eastern Railway, C.B. Fawcett B. Litt., Reader in Geography at Leeds University, wrote of Middlesbrough: "It came in a period when there was no conception of town planning, and so far as its development is concerned, it may be said, like the British Empire, to have been founded in a fit of absence of mind, and then left to look after itself."

Coal traffic continued to grow and it soon outstripped Port Darlington which, being situated on the river bank was, like Stockton, at the mercy of silting and varying water levels caused by the tides. The Middlesbrough Owners, as the consortium was known, put up the money for a new deep water dock where water levels could be controlled by an entrance lock from the river. This was Middlesbrough Dock, complete with 10 coal staithes and a connecting railway from the Port Darlington line. The dock was transferred to S&D ownership in 1849 and over the years was extended several times until it covered 25 acres of water up to 34ft deep. It had a complex internal rail system and until 1937 ships were manoeuvred by railway-owned tugs.

When the railway age began, the region's main port was Whitby, its importance being centred mainly on whaling, but it was also busy with fish and minerals. Looking at the local topography, it is easy to see the difficulty there must have been in moving goods between Whitby and its hinterland. This must have been an issue for local businessmen who looked to the railway for salvation. They backed the Whitby & Pickering Railway, an economy version following the River Esk inland to Grosmont before heading south to Pickering via Goathland. The first stretch to Grosmont opened in June 1835, the rest - including a 1 in 15 rope-hauled passenger incline between Beckhole and Goathland - following 11 months later. Trains were no more than a coach and horses on rails but they did avoid treacherous roads. In 1845 the York & North Midland Railway completed its York-Scarborough line along with a branch from

Cleveland's first railway was still very active in 2007. This is Middlesbrough goods yard, originally Port Darlington, where Type 5 No. 56068 removes potash empties to Boulby at 12.15 on 3rd March 2003.
The passenger station was off to the right and the riverside wharves straight ahead, one line still continuing to such a wharf identified by the distant crane right of the cement silo. To the left used to be a mass of iron and steel works and a short line still goes to the former Ayrton rolling mills, now used as a distribution terminal by A. V. Dawson Ltd.

Stephen Chapman

Rillington, near Malton, to Pickering. It also took over the W&P, creating a through route from Whitby to York and far beyond as well as converting the line to locomotive operation. In 1865 the YNMR's successor, the North Eastern Railway, eliminated the Beckhole incline by opening a new locomotive line up a 1in 49 gradient from Grosmont to Goathland. The original line was retained for goods traffic as far as Beckhole, and from 1908 to 1914 it carried a summer season passenger service.

C. B. Fawcett had this to say about the Whitby-Malton line: "The small population of the areas it connects and its sharp curves and gradients make it of little value." This had not been the view of the YNMR's chairman - the Railway King George Hudson - who immediately saw Whitby's potential as a resort. He began developing the West Cliff area with large houses and the Royal Hotel. Alas, when Hudson fell from grace his half-finished scheme was abandoned and the property eventually sold off.

Having outlined the early beginnings of Cleveland's railways, we can now explore them by joining an imaginary railtour as it might have been at the height of the network in, say, 1910.

Entering Yorkshire from the Stockton direction, we cross the River Tees and pass through Thornaby station. To our left, between the railway and the river, are foundries and engineering works while on the right, a tramway leads to the North Riding Malt House and its adjacent brewery. Further over, on reclaimed Mandale Marshes, is Stockton racecourse.

We then swing away from the river to circumvent the new Erimus hump marshalling yards before crossing over the old River Tees, replaced a hundred years ago by a new cut to remove a large horseshoe bend in the river. After the bridge, sandwiched between us and the river comes Newport engine shed and marshalling yards. The locomotives on shed are hidden by rows of wagons in the sidings occupying the foreground while a P2 class 0-6-0 which has run on the goods line alongside us since Thornaby station leads its coal train into the yards. Newport yards were established in 1875, the S&D line on which we are travelling being diverted inland from the river to make room for them. They stretch for almost a mile until we reach Newport station.

For the next half mile we run alongside Newport ironworks and rolling mills to reach Old Town Junction. Here the original S&D line goes straight on under a road bridge to what is now Middlesbrough goods station. There it fans out to serve riverside wharves while to its west a mass of sidings extend like some creeping weed into a vast conurbation of iron works, blast furnaces and related

Class A5 4-6-2T No. 69832 circumvents Newport yards(left)via the passenger lines with a 1950s Saltburn to Darlington train formed of the articulated suburban stock commonly used on this service at the time. When Tees yard was built, two new footbridges over the diverted passenger lines utilised wrought iron spans recovered from Cockfield Fell(near Barnard Castle) and Hare Park(Wakefield) *Peter Cookson collection*

industries occupying a peninsular formed by a large bend in the river. They include the Acklam, Ayresome, Linthorpe and West Marsh iron works, Britannia iron and steel works, Newport wire works, North Eastern steel works and Ayrton rolling mills - no wonder people call it the Ironmasters' District. The Marsh branch, which left the goods lines near Newport iron works, serves many of these plants.

Curving away from Old Town along the extension opened c.1842 to serve Middlesbrough dock we soon enter the arched trainshed of Middlesbrough station. Immediately upon leaving, we are presented with a breathtaking vista of railways and shipping. On the left, lines spread out into the docks area with all its cranes, coal tipplers, ships' funnels and masts while on the right are the three roundhouses that make up Middlesbrough engine shed. In front of the shed is Guisborough Junction where the line to Guisborough and Battersby heads away southwards. Out of sight, beyond Old Town and the docks, a goods railway runs along the south bank of the river. Now part of the NER, it was originally the Middlesbrough Owner's Railway stretching from Old Town to Cargo Fleet, serving numerous wharves, factories and the docks on its way.

We are now on the S&D's Middlesbrough & Redcar Railway(opened 1846) and for much of the way, the great black steaming edifices of iron works, blast furnaces, coking plants and steel mills close in on both sides. Everywhere, amongst these plants are their attendant railways weaving here and there with small locomotives shuffling about pushing and pulling wagons or ladles of steaming slag fresh from the furnaces. Soon after the docks, we see Pease & Partners' Tees iron works on the south bank of the river, followed immediately by Cochranes' Ormesby iron works as we pass Cargo Fleet station. After crossing two creeks we see Normanby iron works and Cargo Fleet Junction as, on the south side, a tramway goes off to a brickworks, followed by Cargo Fleet iron works where the Normanby branch diverges away. Originally the Cleveland Railway, opened in stages during the 1860s, it went 15 miles to ironstone mines near Loftus but after being taken over by the NER in 1865, the middle section between Normanby and just beyond Guisborough was abandoned and the mines served by other lines. The branch now only carries local passenger trains to Eston as well as serving Normanby and Ormesby mines, and Normanby brickworks with its 600-yard incline descending 400ft from a clay pit on Upsall Moor. Shortly after Cargo Fleet salt works on the river side, the Cleveland line passes overhead to reach a jetty for ferrying ironstone across the river to Bell Brothers' ironworks at Port Clarence.

The next mile is punctuated only by South Bank station and a nearby brick and tile works until we approach Grangetown and the sprawling mass of Bolckow & Vaughan's Cleveland works, the biggest we will encounter. First, on the south side, are the six Clay Lane furnaces followed the five Cleveland furnaces and then the steel works. From sidings between the two banks of furnaces, another branch disappears south and heads for the hills. This is the Eston Mines Railway, a 2.5-mile iron company's line built for moving ironstone from the mines around Eston to Cleveland works. The branch was opened in 1850 by the works' owners and includes a line extending underneath ours to reach the eight massive South Bank blast furnaces which tower over us on the river side like the skyscrapers of the New World. At Eston, three inclines come down from mines in the hills, one of them part of a two-mile tramway along Lackenby Bank. The Eston iron mines are reputed to be the most productive in the world. A limited passenger service ran along this line until the NER began its own operation in 1902.

Following Grangetown station a smaller iron works is on the south side of the line at North Lackenby. It has its own internal line crossing under ours to slag tipping grounds on the riverside mudflats.With marshland on both sides, the next two thirds of a mile are broken only by Lazenby Siding until we reach Tod Point, where the Tees meets the North Sea. Here, Redcar iron works stands on the south side and Coatham ironworks on the river side. An industrial tramway leading from Redcar works to the South Gare breakwater and Redcar jetty passes over us immediately east of the works.

As our line curves past Warrenby a long siding goes straight on to end with the earthworks of an abandoned railway - remains of the original Middlesbrough & Redcar line, the Redcar end having been replaced by the 1861 extension to Saltburn which we have now joined. Along with the rest of the S&D, this line was absorbed by the NER in 1863. Next comes Redcar, a through station which replaced the Middlesbrough & Redcar terminus when the present line was built. In open country, about a mile further on are Upleatham sidings and the junction with a branch going south to the Derwent Iron company's Upleatham mine. Marske station is next and then Saltburn Extension Junction where the line up to Brotton, and ultimately Whitby, climbs away to the south.

Saltburn terminus is dominated by the Zetland Hotel, standing at the very end of the line. Built by

Where great black steaming edifices close in on both sides. This British Railways photo shows the scene looking east at Cargo Fleet Junction with the lines into the works leading under the footbridge.
Ken Appleby collection

the railway with an eye on turning the then fishing hamlet into a holiday resort, it has its own platform so that well-to-do guests swapping industrial smog for fresh sea air, can step straight from the hotel's grand opulence into their first class compartments.

Back at Middlesbrough, we now travel south along the Middlesbrough & Guisborough Railway, opened to passengers in 1854 and absorbed by the S&D in 1857. Immediately upon leaving Guisborough Junction are Toll Bar sidings serving Sadler's chemical works in the 'V' with the Saltburn line, and the Linthorpe branch of the Middlesbrough Owners' Railway going off to the west, one of its nearer sidings serving some brine wells. The line then swaps the industrial confines of Middlesbrough for open country as it passes through Ormesby station and climbs for well over a mile at 1 in 40 between the estates of Marton and Ormesby halls to reach Nunthorpe station. After just over another mile comes Nunthorpe East Junction where the Battersby branch curves away to the south west. As we turn towards Guisborough, the 1049ft sugar loaf Roseberry Topping stands on our right as the pinacle of the Cleveland Hills. Some say that mining subsidence and erosion are causing the hill to change shape. Just before Pinchinthorpe, a rusty branch diverges north east to Bolckow & Vaughan's Chaloner iron mine just over two miles away. It was laid in 1873 to replace the 1860s Cleveland Railway connection but it is now little used as the output goes via the Eston Mines Railway. Then, going south east, are the earthworks of another old line, this one up to Codhill mine on the edge of Guisborough Moor; it closed in the 1860s, despite being the original purpose of this railway from Middlesbrough. Just after Hutton Gate station the Belmont mine branch diverges in a south easterly direction then, three and three quarter miles from Nunthorpe East, we reach Hutton Junction. From here the M&G line terminates half a mile further on at Guisborough station, but we keep going along the line opened in 1862 to connect the M&G with the Cleveland. Hutton Junction faces west so trains entering the station from the east have to reverse in.

Continuing eastwards, we eventually see the short branch to Spa Wood mine heading away south. Soon after that we pass over the 60ft-high Waterfall Viaduct, its eight 40ft spans bringing us to Slapewath. Until recently this was a busy junction where several mines branches met the main line. Now, only the line north to Skelton and Skelton Park mines and another south to Stanghow mine, remain active, other branches going south to Slapewath and Ayesdalegate mines having closed a few years ago. We really are in iron mining country now and between here and Boosbeck station we pass the big

South Skelton mine. East of Boosbeck comes Priestcroft Junction where a spur drops away northwards at 1 in 55 to pass North Skelton mine and join the Brotton-Saltburn line, opened by the NER in 1872. Descending at 1 in 72/70, it passes North Skelton station, Longacre mine and crosses towering Skelton Beck viaduct to reach Saltburn Extension Junction. Our journey continues along the Brotton line to Kiltonthorpe Junction. Here, another goods branch goes south to Lingdale Junction where it divides to serve Kilton and Lingdale mines. Lumpsey mine comes next, in the 'V' of the junction with the Saltburn line just outside Brotton. At Brotton station we pass a Saltburn to Guisborough 'autocar', its 0-4-4 Bogie Tank Passenger locomotive sandwiched between the driving carriages. It has to reverse three times during its journey.

Still on the old Cleveland line, we press on from Brotton, rounding a headland on the very edge of perilous cliffs before coming to Crag Hall and Skinningrove where the iron works overlooks the sea. On the same side, a goods line descends sharply alongside us and into Skinningrove village which nestles in the ravine we are now crossing on the curving 150ft-high Kilton Viaduct, its wrought iron superstructure supported by 12 stone piers. So steep is the goods line's descent to reach Loftus mine way below that it has to zig-zag its way down by two reverse junctions, the first right under the viaduct and the second in the centre of the village. Mining subsidence is affecting the viaduct so badly that in 1908 the NER secured an Act of Parliament which will enable it to convert the viaduct into an embankment using spoil from the nearby mines.

Over the viaduct, the 10 furnaces of Liverton iron works are on the west side of the line as we approach Loftus station and join what started out as the Whitby, Redcar & Middlesbrough Union Railway. From here, we face a precarious route along the cliff tops to Whitby, crossing five ravines and inlets along the way, each requiring an ironwork viaduct of substantial height and length. To build a railway along such a route would have tested any company but the independent and hard-up WR&MU got into serious difficulty. Rockfalls, collapsing cliffs and a shortage of money resulted in cheapskate workmanship which became manifest in weak and dangerous viaducts. In 1875, nine years after first being authorized by Parliament, the NER took over the work and did not complete it until December 1883, after having to rebuild or strengthen several major structures.

The line is single track but all stations except Sandsend have passing loops. Through the 993-yard Grinkle Tunnel we descend at 1 in 61 past ironstone mines on both sides of the line at Boulby to rejoin the sea at the fishing village of Staithes. Approaching

Staithes Viaduct, the biggest of several major structures on the coastal route between Loftus and Whitby stood 152ft tall at its highest point and had six 60ft and eleven 30ft spans. Here, BR Standard Class 4 2-6-4T No. 80116 rumbles a Whitby-bound service towards the station in May 1958. *Ken. Hoole / N. Stead collection*

the station we cross a viaduct so high and exposed that it is fitted with a device which rings a bell in the signal box when the wind becomes too strong. The trains are then stopped and the viaduct inspected before they are allowed to resume.

About a mile after Staithes, a busy 3ft gauge tramway passes unseen beneath us. Underground at this point, it connects Palmers' mines in Grinkle Park with Port Mulgrave where it emerges suddenly from the cliff face onto a tall jetty where the ironstone is tipped into barges. Inland, it winds its way in the open through secluded glades and valleys all the way back to the mine we passed on the south side of the line at Boulby.

After crossing a northbound train at Hinderwell but nothing in the loop at Kettleness we pass through the 308-yard Kettleness Tunnel and then, with the sea down below, quickly come up against Sandsend Ness headland. The original line went round the cliff face - no wonder it fell into the sea. The line as finally built by the NER takes us down a 1 in 57 gradient and through a 1652-yard tunnel to emerge amidst a barren expanse of old alum workings in the narrow space between us and the sea as we descend to Sandsend. Through the single line station and over the viaduct, we then rumble across East Row viaduct

with the fine beach way below us to pass East Row goods shed. With our engine working hard up the 1 in 60 to Whitby, we cross Newholme Beck and Upgang viaducts on the way.

In a cutting just after West Cliff station, we meet the Scarborough & Whitby line at Prospect Hill Junction where the signal box straddles the single track down to Whitby Town as the Scarborough line, consisting at this point of a single track and crossing loop, heads straight on. We snake our way down the north face of the Esk Valley to join the Whitby & Pickering line at the charmingly named Bog Hall Junction for the short run past the engine shed and goods yards into Whitby Town.

The final leg of our excursion takes us along the double track Whitby & Pickering line which follows the north bank of the River Esk. The estuary here is in a wide but deep gorge and after Bog Hall Junction and the gas works, we pass under the elegant Larpool Viaduct carrying the Scarborough & Whitby Railway over the valley. Opened in 1885, the S&WR was an independent concern worked by the NER which took it over in 1898.

Immediately after Ruswarp station, we cross to the south side of the Esk - the first of 18 crossings we will make of the river in the next 13 miles. After Sleights

About to take the Battersby line at Grosmont Junction on 12th May 1984 is a Deltic Preservation Society special returning from Whitby to King's Cross hauled Brush Type 4 No. 47323. To the left of the loco is the ground frame controlling access to the North Yorkshire Moors Railway since the closure of Grosmont signal box in 1972. The overbridge has since been dismantled. *Stephen Chapman*

station, we pass Harrison's Woodlands Siding on the north side and Gantree Siding on the south side as well as Newbiggn Siding before reaching Grosmont where the line continues south through the station's Pickering platforms and into Grosmont Tunnel. We curve round along the Grosmont & Castleton branch, opened by the NER in 1865. By meeting the North Yorkshire & Cleveland Railway at Castleton, it provides a through route between Whitby and the Leeds Northern main line running from Leeds to Newcastle via Stockton. The first section of the NY&CR, to Stokesley from its junction with the Leeds Northern at Picton, was opened in 1857 and the final stretch to Castleton in 1861, two years after the NER had taken it over.

The single track to Castleton leaves its own platform at the 'V'-shaped Grosmont station where directly opposite loomed Grosmont ironworks, closed around 1891. Its three blast furnaces were fed by a tramway descending over the main line from mines in the hills opposite. Esk Valley ironstone is reputed to have been discovered during construction of the Whitby & Pickering line which then prospered by conveying the ore to Whitby for shipping to Tyneside.

From Egton we regularly swap sides with the now tumbling Esk until reaching Glaisdale and the first crossing loop. After the station was another iron-works, on the south side of the line, again fed by an inclined tramway from mines in the moor but it lasted only from 1866 to 1875. In a field on the north side a meaningless stone overbridge marks the aborted Cleveland Extension Mineral Railway from Lingdale - also known as Paddy Waddell's railway after its contractor. Started in the 1870s, it was at first intended for moving ironstone to Glaisdale but construction ceased when only a few earthworks had been built. Beyond the bridge we can easily look down upon the unused embankment which stops abruptly at the river.

Enjoying the Esk Valley's tranquil beauty, we pass through Lealhom station, and then Danby with its goods loop, before reaching the next loop at Castleton Moor. Commondale, where a short branch crosses the river and goes northwards to a brickworks, is next. Just under two miles after Kildale, where narrow gauge lines once came down from nearby mines, we join the single line from Nunthorpe and run into Battersby station. Instigated by the North Yorkshire

& Cleveland, the Nunthorpe branch was opened as a goods line by the NER in 1864 and passenger services did not begin until 1868, its original purpose being to speed the movement of ironstone to Middlesbrough. The only intermediate station and crossing loop is at Great Ayton but there, in the space of a mile, is a cluster of ironstone mines and whinstone quarries served by standard and narrow gauge railways and inclines.

Next to Battersby station, the 14-mile line to Rosedale mines diverges away in a southerly direction. Alongside is an engine shed built to provide locomotives for the Rosedale traffic but now closed. The Rosedale line opened in 1861 and follows the course of a narrow gauge line built in 1858 by the Ingleby Mining Co. to its mines at Ingleby Greenhow. From there it ascends a rope-worked incline - 1 in 5 at its steepest - to the moors where it continues across the tops at well over 1000ft above sea level to the mines and calcining kilns that roast the ore(to make it lighter and cheaper to move) at West Rosedale. A branch to East Rosedale serves mines there along with general goods and coal depots. Railway employees live with their families in their own village at West Rosedale where an engine shed houses the locomotives that work in isolation to the top of the incline.

From Battersby we progress along double track through farmland past Ingleby, Stokesley, Sexhow, Potto and Trenholme Bar stations before reaching Picton to join the Leeds Northern line. On the approach to Potto a recently lifted branch comes in from the south. Opened in 1857, it served Whorlton mines two miles away but like many of the ironstone mines, inland iron works and railways built to serve them, it barely outlived the 19th century.

Passenger services

Cleveland's main passenger artery has always been the line through Middlesbrough to Redcar and Saltburn. It carries Teesside's busiest passenger trains, namely those which run between Saltburn and Darlington - and it is interesting to note that by 2006 the service pattern and intensity had remained broadly similar for over 60 years.

The summer 1950 timetable showed 35 mainly half-hourly weekday trains from Darlington to Saltburn (departing Middlesbrough 5.25am to 11.38pm) and 33 from Saltburn(departing 5.1am to 11pm.) There was a good Sunday service too and in the 1950s it included a through summer train each way to and from Penrith via the Stainmore line. The summer 2006 timetable showed 28 weekday trains to Saltburn(departing Middlesbrough 6.34am to 10.9pm) and 29 from Saltburn(departing 6.24am to 10.40pm.) Apart the few trains not covering the whole route and odd ones between Saltburn and

Potto, on the North Yorkshire & Cleveland line, was a typical North Eastern country station. Class G5 0-4-4T No. 67343, from 51C West Hartlepool shed, arrives with a Stockton to Whitby train in the early 1950s. *J.W. Armstrong Trust.*

Stockton, the main variations to the basic service were London trains. In summer 1950 they comprised the 7.7am Mondays, Fridays, Saturdays only and 7.53am weekdays Saltburn to King's Cross through carriages via Stockton, and the 5.35pm through carriages from King's Cross which were attached to the 10.23pm from Darlington, reaching Saltburn at 11.21pm. Through carriages provided a direct link between Saltburn and King's Cross until the 1960s and by 1955 they included a late Friday evening service to London. For a time there were also through trains: the 7.5am Saltburn-King's Cross(6.5 on Sats.) and the 2pm return(4.20 on Sats.), as in summer 1960. The summer 1955 working timetable declared that notice had to be given the previous day if any passengers wished to join the 7.50am Saltburn-King's Cross through carriages at Marske.

Teesside's next most important service ran between Middlesbrough, Stockton and Newcastle via the Durham coast. Once again, today's service pattern remains similar to that at the start of the 1950s with through trains at roughly hourly intervals. During the 1950s, there were a dozen weekday Middlesbrough-Newcastle trains each way while a few more ran between Middlesbrough and West Hartlepool, providing connections at Stockton with coast line expresses to/from such places as Liverpool

and Colchester. Middlesbrough/Thornaby- Haverton Hill workers' trains also used part of this route. In summer 1955, by which time this Monday-Friday service was no longer advertised in the public timetable, trains left Thornaby at 6.31 and 6.55am and Haverton Hill for Middlesbrough at 4.34pm(unadvertised before Billingham) and 5.15pm(unadvertised before Stockton.)

Direct services between Middlesbrough and the south via Northallerton were sparse. The only normal weekday service trains in the summer 1950 timetable were the 9.17am Leeds-Middlesbrough which arrived at 11.47, and the 12.55pm Middlesbrough-Northallerton. There were more by summer 1960: the 7.52am Leeds-Middlesbrough diesel multiple unit and 2pm(4.20 Sats.) King's Cross-Saltburn, the 7.5am(6.5 Sats.) Saltburn-King's Cross plus the 6.50am Middlesbrough-York and 11.20am Middlesbrough-Harrogate DMUs.

Cleveland's remaining passenger services comprised four different routes to Whitby. During the 1950s, the main one was provided by Middlesbrough-Scarborough trains taking the spectacular coastal route via Guisborough, Staithes, Whitby West Cliff and Robin Hood's Bay. Trains from Middlesbrough calling at Guisborough had to reverse back out of the terminus to the junction before continuing to Whitby

One of the few regular passenger trains to run directly between Middlesbrough and Northallerton during the 1950s. Northallerton's D20/1 4-4-0 No. 62347 rolls into Thornaby station with what may well be the 12.55pm Middlesbrough-Northallerton. *K. H. Cockerill/J. W. Armstrong Trust*

At what was originally Hutton Junction, A8 4-6-2T No. 69880 takes the Middlesbrough & Guisborough line into Guisborough station with a Middlesbrough-Whitby train in August 1955. Upon leaving Guisborough, 69880 will have to propel its train back to the junction before continuing forward along the line in the foreground which was laid in 1862 to connect the M&G with the Cleveland Railway to Loftus.
The signal box here was renamed Guisborough following closure of the box at Guisborough station during the 1930s, and the double track into Guisborough worked as two single lines, one for passenger and one for goods.
J.W. Armstrong Trust

while those towards Middlesbrough had to reverse from the junction into the terminus. There was another reversal to perform at Scarborough as the junction with the Whitby line faced away from the Central station.

In summer 1946, Guisborough enjoyed no less than 12 trains to and eleven from Middlesbrough each weekday plus an extra each way on Saturday evenings. Of these, two each way ran to and from Whitby and two each way to and from Scarborough. The first trains on a weekday were the 5.5am Guisborough-Middlesbrough and the 6.15am Middlesbrough-Scarborough, and the last trains the 4.33pm Scarborough-Middlesbrough(the 8pm from Guisborough on Saturdays) and the 7.15pm Middlesbrough-Guisborough(8.50pm on Sats.) The Sunday service consisted of one Whitby and one Scarborough train each way.

By summer 1957, Guisborough's weekday service was much reduced, comprising the 9.7am and 12.32pm Middlesbrough-Whitby, 4.20pm Middlesbrough-Scarborough,5.18pm Middlesbrough-Guisborough, 7am and 6.33pm Whitby-Middlesbrough, 11.40am and 4.27pm Scarborough-Middlesbrough and 7.59pm Scarborough-Stockton (West Hartlepool in high summer), plus an extra Middlesbrough-Guisborough train each way on

Saturdays and an extra midweek Middlesbrough-Whitby train each way in high summer. The weekdays 8.2am Darlington-Scarborough, 9.44am and 10.45am(high summer) Middlesbrough-Scarborough all missed Guisborough, the latter calling at Hutton Gate. The 8.2 Darlington-Scarborough was fastest at the time, running non-stop from Middlesbrough to Staithes and covering the whole 58-miles from Middlesbrough to Scarborough in 2 hours 14 minutes. Most other trains could take up to three hours. In summer 2006 the Middlesbrough to Scarborough journey could routinely be achieved in around two hours but with tight connections at Darlington and York, two hours 38 minutes being more usual.

More Middlesbrough-Whitby trains ran via Redcar and Brotton and until 1933 the Whitby service ran from Saltburn. In summer 1946 two southbound and three northbound Teesside-Scarborough trains used the Saltburn-Brotton line on summer Saturdays. On each weekday, two trains each way (remnants of services past) provided connections between Brotton(for Guisborough line trains) and Saltburn, calling at North Skelton and reversing at Saltburn West Junction. Formed of push-pull stock or Sentinel steam railcars, they left Saltburn at 9.50am and 6.17pm and Brotton at 10.35am and 6.50pm.

The summer 1950 timetable showed the Saltburn

Brotton station looking east in July 1938 with Sentinel steam railcar *Neptune* forming the Guisborough-Saltburn shuttle. Brotton's impressive red brick buildings survive in 2007. *N. Stead collection*

West-Brotton line again carrying a full weekday service. The Brotton-Saltburn shuttle had ceased, Saltburn passengers being advised to change at Marske or Redcar East. The weekday service comprised the 8.15am Eaglescliffe-Scarborough, 10.38am Middlesbrough-Scarborough and 7.55pm Middlesbrough-Whitby, the 10am Whitby-Middlesbrough, the 5.10pm(summer dated) and 5.50pm Scarborough-Middlesbrough, and the 6.25pm(summer dated) Scarborough-Stockton, all but the Eaglescliffe and Stockton trains calling at North Skelton. Middlesbrough-Scarborough journey times were similar to those via Guisborough, the fastest northbound being the 6.25pm Scarborough-Stockton, taking 2 hours 31 minutes. North Skelton closed to passengers on 15th January 1951 when the local service was withdrawn but reopened for the summer season, finally closing on 10th September. After that, only summer dated weekday passenger trains travelled this way: in summer 1955 the 8.20 and 10am Stockton-Scarborough, the 5.50pm Scarborough-West Hartlepool and the 6.28pm Scarborough-Stockton. The service remained similar until summer 1957 after which the Loftus-Whitby closure put an end to it.

At Whitby, Middlesbrough-Scarborough trains used West Cliff station with connections for the more central Whitby Town. The summer 1946 timetable shows connections maintained entirely by Middlesbrough-Whitby Town and Scarborough-Whitby Town services but during the 1950s, additional shuttle trains ran between the two stations, taking six minutes. In summer 1955 they consisted of seven each way, eight on Saturdays. After that, two-coach winter service Middlesbrough-Scarborough trains were permitted to serve both Whitby Town and West Cliff by propelling between the two - giving some trains five reversals during their journey.

Whitby's third link with Teesside was to Stockton via Battersby and Picton. In summer 1950 it saw just two through weekday trains from Whitby, at 6.45am and 5.50pm, both calling all stations and taking over two hours to complete their journeys. In the other direction were the 7.15 and 10am Stockton-Whitby, 3.35pm West Hartlepool-Whitby and the 6pm Stockton-Battersby. There was no Sunday service between Picton and Battersby and services on this section were withdrawn from 14th June 1954.

The fourth route to Whitby was a mere branch line via Nunthorpe and Battersby but it became the sole survivor ultimately providing Whitby's only link to the national rail network. Always a lifeline for the isolated communities of the Esk Valley, especially when local roads are blocked by snow, its services have traditionally included trains timed specifically for pupils attending school in Whitby. In summer 1950, its weekday service amounted to just two Middlesbrough to Whitby trains plus the 7.57am (Saturdays excepted) Kildale-Whitby and the 7.19am Middlesbrough-Battersby which connected with the 7.15 Stockton-Whitby. Three ran from Whitby while the 8.10am and 7.20pm Battersby-Middlesbrough provided connections off Whitby-Stockton trains. A summer Sunday service of two out and back Whitby trains ran for day trippers. With the Picton line service gone, the number of trains via Nunthorpe was increased. In summer 1957 there were four weekday trains each way(including the 9.42am Stockton-Whitby) plus an extra midweek out and back day trip working from Middlesbrough in high summer, an extra each way on Saturdays, the 7.57am Saturdays excepted   Battersby-Whitby, 4.5pm return and 5.30pm back to Whitby, and the 9.5pm Saturdays Only Whitby-Glaisdale. The first Whitby train left Middlesbrough at 8.7am(7.38 on Saturdays), and Whitby for Middlesbrough at 6.49am. The last train from Middlesbrough was at 6.5pm and from Whitby to Middlesbrough at 8.35pm. Between Grosmont and

Whitby the service was augmented by Pickering trains. Lines south of Whitby will hopefully be the subject of a future Railway Memories so suffice it to say that the origins and destinations of trains on this route varied according to seasonal and local requirements. Like the Esk Valley it was also a lifeline for local communities, saw trains run for the benefit of schoolchildren and included two trains each way purely between Goathland and Whitby. The basic service was between Malton and Whitby but in the summer season trains ran to or from York, Leeds and on certain days through carriages were conveyed to/from King's Cross. The Middlesbrough trains made up most of the Whitby-Scarborough service but extra trains ran purely between Whitby Town and Scarborough, reversing at West Cliff; four such trains ran each way in summer 1957.

Although before the Railway Memories era, it is worth mentioning for the record one other passenger service which operated in Cleveland, from 1902 to 1929. This ran between Middlesbrough and Eston where the NER built a small station with single-storey wooden buildings at the end of a short branch off the former Cleveland Railway at Flatts Lane. Five trains ran each way in 1910 plus extras on Wednesday evenings and Saturdays. Cargo Fleet was the only intermediate stop and the four and three

Battersby at 1.22pm on 16th April 1958. With the disused engine shed on the left, L1 2-6-4T No. 67766 of 51D Middlesbrough shed, is ready to depart after running round its train, the 12.5pm Whitby-Middlesbrough. Three weeks later this became the only route between Middlesbrough and Whitby. *David Holmes*

quarter-mile journey took 15 minutes.

In September 1957, diesel multiple units started to replace steam on virtually all local services in the area, the changeover being fully implemented on 5th May 1958. They brought many improvements and were popular with passengers due to their new, clean environment and much improved view of the local scenery. The Darlington-Saltburn line benefitted mainly from a slight cut in end-to-end journey times to around an hour while the service pattern was regularized and the number of weekday trains slightly increased to 39 each way. As a result, the number of passenger journeys rose by 28 per cent in the first year to 3,623,221 and receipts by 40 per cent to £182,441. Remaining loco-hauled local trains in the summer 1960 working timetable were the 4.30am and 10.11pm(10.40 on Sats) from Darlington, the latter conveying through carriages from King's Cross, and the 7.40am Saturdays Only Saltburn-Stockton.

The Middlesbrough-Newcastle weekday service was increased to 16 trains running throughout each way, leaving Middlesbrough at mainly 36 minutes past the hour in summer 1960 but with little reduction in overall journey times. The remaining Middlesbrough-Haverton Hill train each way was also a DMU until its eventual demise. The 5.5am

from Newcastle, and 12.35am Saturdays Only and 6.5am Stockton-Middlesbrough stayed loco-hauled.

Diesel traction wasn't new to the Middlesbrough-Scarborough route as the LNER tried a prototype railcar on the winter service, but the advent of DMUs undoubtably influenced the timing of the Whitby-Loftus closure on 5th May 1958. The ease with which they could reverse direction compared with steam enabled Middlesbrough-Scarborough trains to be re-routed via Battersby and Whitby Town - with reversals at Battersby, Whitby Town, West Cliff and Scarborough. The DMUs brought the best ever Esk Valley line service and the summer 1960 working timetable showed nine weekday trains from Middlesbrough to Whitby(two starting from Darlington and all but one continuing to Scarborough) plus four more on Saturdays(daily in high summer.) Overall journey times were around two and a half hours even with four reversals but the 9.50am West Hartlepool-Scarborough which did not call at West Cliff, reversing instead at Prospect Hill, covered the 58.5 miles in 2 hours 7 minutes. In the other direction, nine DMUs ran from Scarborough to Middlesbrough with two more starting from Whitby. On Saturdays, one extra train ran from Scarborough and one extra from Whitby. Besides these, one

Between 1957 and 1958 diesel multiple units took over just about all local services in Cleveland, rendering the A8s and other steam passenger tanks redundant. Just before the diesel takeover, two Derby Lightweight 4-car sets(E79150 leading) approach Redcar Central with a Newcastle-Saltburn special on 10th June 1957. The number 53 carried on the front was, intriguingly, the Working Timetable number for a Sunderland-King's Cross train. *Neville Stead collection*

Monday-Saturday plus one Saturday Only Scarborough-Whitby train ran each way.

The Loftus-Whitby closure left a rump service of four Middlesbrough-Guisborough-Loftus DMUs each way on weekdays plus another three each way between Middlesbrough and Guisborough, one of which formed an additional service to Loftus and back on Saturdays. By summer 1959, the Loftus service was down to just three each way on weekdays plus the Saturday extra.

DMUs were introduced on the Whitby-Malton line in 1959 but steam kept a foothold - the most notable change here by 1960 being that most trains now ran between Whitby and York. Parcels and mail traffic, heavy summer loadings and through workings meant that some trains remained loco-hauled. One example was the summer 1960 10.28am from York, loco-hauled on Saturdays but a DMU midweek except from 4th July to 26th August when the working timetable specified "worked by steam."

The 1960s were notorious for the Beeching Axe and especially so in this part of the world, not just because his closure plan would have wiped Whitby off the rail map but also because Dr. Beeching was a senior executive with Teesside-based ICI before and after his chairmanship of British Railways. That memorable decade began with closure of Loftus, Brotton and Boosbeck stations on 2nd May 1960, leaving just five Middlesbrough-Guisborough trains each way in the summer 1960 working timetable. Another pre-Beeching casualty was Whitby West Cliff, closed on 12th June 1961 from which date all Scarborough trains reversed at Prospect Hill. Guisborough became the first Beeching casualty, losing its passenger service on 2nd March 1964.

Beeching proposed closing all the remaining lines to Whitby. Fierce opposition was swept aside by BR and government but the minister of transport did finally refuse closure of the Battersby route, although its long-term future was far from certain. Services from Malton and Scarborough ceased from 8th March 1965, to leave the passenger network we know today. Whitby's holiday trade was badly hit by these closures. The Yorkshire Post reported that whereas the mid-morning summer Saturday Whitby-York train carried on average 300 passengers in 1964, the replacement bus on 14th August 1965 carried just two beyond Goathland. Throughout the Beeching era, BR and its government masters showed no desire to cut costs in order to keep lines open, but the climate changed with the 1968 Transport Act and the introduction of annual "Grant Aid" subsidies. In 1969 the Whitby branch was awarded £208,000 government support but in return BR was required to make severe economies. One of these was the introduction that same year of the now

routine Paytrain system where stations are unstaffed and guards issue tickets on the trains. The Darlington-Saltburn service was awarded £348,000 in 1969 and Middlesbrough-Newcastle £343,000 per year for 1969 and 1970.

After closure, both the Whitby-Pickering and Scarborough lines became subject to preservation bids. Ultimately, it was the Pickering line which succeeded as a mainly steam-operated railway. The North Yorkshire Moors Railway first ran trains between Grosmont and Ellerbeck, the whole line to Pickering reopening officially in 1973. Since then it has become one of Britain's leading heritage railways, making a significant contribution to the local economy while many hope that before long its trains will run throughout between Pickering and Whitby.

Serving three major seaside resorts plus Stockton and Redcar races, Cleveland's railways saw many extra trains on summer Saturdays and bank holidays besides the normal services already mentioned. During the 1950s they included trains from Glasgow, Blackpool, Southport, King's Cross and Leeds to Redcar and Saltburn with associated return workings, empty stock and light engine movements. Certain Newcastle-Middlesbrough trains were extended to/from Redcar while extra summer Saturday trains ran to and from Whitby and Scarborough via the Guisborough, Redcar and, from 1958, Battersby routes. Extra trains also came to Whitby from York and Leeds via Malton. Summer brought the memorable scenic specials allowing holidaymakers to enjoy the North Yorkshire Moors and coastline. Such excursions came from the West Riding - heavy trains double-headed to cope with the stiff Whitby-Scarborough gradients - while there was a midweek Scarborough-Rillington-Whitby-Scarborough circular tour for Scarborough holidaymakers. These seaside specials faded away during the 1960s, killed off by line closures, overseas package holidays, car ownership and BR economies, including a cull of the coaching stock fleet and abandonment of facilities for handling such traffic.

A number of parcels trains(eight on weekdays in 1955) plied between Saltburn, Middlesbrough, Stockton and Darlington, often calling at many intermediate stations. They included the 11.52pm Darlington-Middlesbrough which provided an unadvertised passenger service when required. Parcels and mail were also carried by normal passenger trains but the DMUs had limited space, underlining the need for dedicated trains. Seven such trains a day still ran along these routes in summer 1969, four of them utilising DMUs authorized to haul up to 250 tons of parcels vans(4-car sets) or 140 tons(2-car sets) but traffic gradually faded due to road competition and industrial decline, and in 1981 BR began pulling out of the parcels business when it withdrew its collect and delivery service. Nowadays the railway carries virtually no parcels in this area.

Post-Beeching, the only BR passenger trains left operating in Cleveland were Darlington-Saltburn, Middlesbrough-Newcastle and Middlesbrough-Whitby. No booked passenger trains ran directly between Middlesbrough and the south via Northallerton. But as in many places, there has been something of a revival since those dark days of the late 1960s and early 1970s.

Between 1981 and 1989 Middlesbrough again had its own direct London service - the early morning and evening return 'Cleveland Executive', formed of a 125mph High Speed Train and providing Pullman-style service to passengers travelling first class. Taking the direct Middlesbrough-Northallerton route, it gave Teesside executives a full day in the capital without having to change at Darlington. A corresponding morning train to Middlesbrough and afternoon return were introduced in June 1981 but had ceased by 1983.

The 1980s saw the 1950s DMUs replaced by new trains, mainly the Pacer railbuses whose mechanical failures are legendary. These failures led to an acute rolling stock shortage and for a time in 1986/87 BR resorted loco-hauled trains on the Middlesbrough-Newcastle service for the first time in 30 years.

Teesside's passenger services were utterly transformed in May 1992 when BR introduced new Middlesbrough-Liverpool TransPennine expresses, bringing regular passenger trains to the direct Northallerton route. Trains ran at roughly two-hour intervals but two years later they were increased to hourly and switched to Manchester Airport to form the service that still runs in 2006. Another upgrade came in May 1994 when fast trains were introduced between Saltburn and Newcastle via Darlington. The two-hourly service pattern didn't last and in 2006 just three early morning trains ran from south Teesside with a 22.00 return from Newcastle.

The Whitby branch has survived but not without pain and the threat of closure has always hung over it like the Sword of Damocles. By summer 1969 its service still stood at six weekday trains each way (including the 05.00 ex-Darlington which was first stop Battersby,) plus one extra each way in high summer, and two more each way on Saturdays. There was also a limited Middlesbrough-Nunthorpe commuter service - a relic of the Guisborough trains. Four Whitby trains ran each way on Sundays. During the mid-1970s, great efforts were made by BR, local authorities and other interested parties to improve the line's viability. It was branded the 'Esk Valley Line' and various marketing initiatives used to drum up business, especially outside the holiday season. Services were improved and the Esk Valley Line Committee set up to support the line and encourage its use. On 3rd May 1976 a new timetable was launched, giving the branch its best service for years, a new halt was opened at Gypsy Lane, between Ormesby and Nunthorpe, and passenger

The desolate scene at Saltburn on 2nd February 1970. All track has been removed from the excursion platform(left) and the main platform leading through the trainshed to the Zetland Hotel, leaving just waste ground as a plain BR corporate blue-liveried Metro-Cammell DMU is sidelined into the bay. Parcels traffic continues over on the right, however. *Neville Stead collection*

When this picture was taken of a Middlesbrough-Whitby 3-car Metro-Cammell DMU at Castleton on 2nd August 1981, the Esk Valley line was again under threat. Within a few years the left hand platform, the signal box, crossing loop and siding had been stripped away and the DMUs replaced by brand new trains, mainly Pacers. *Neville Stead*

loadings doubled by the end of the year. The May 1978-May 1979 timetable showed seven weekday trains each way plus two more each way during the summer, and a vibrant commuter service backed by Cleveland County Council of six trains from Middlesbrough to Nunthorpe and eleven from Nunthorpe. Five Whitby trains ran each way on summer Sundays.

The line came under renewed threat in 1981 when BR's Eastern Region declared loudly and publicly that without increased government investment and despite massive economies and increased patronage, 36 branch lines would face closure due to the worn out state of trains, track and signalling - and it held up the Whitby line as the prime example. "Ten years ago the Whitby line was staffed by 30 people, now it is run by six," said general manager Frank Paterson. Within just a few years, however, the old DMUs were replaced,albeit by Pacers, signalling ultimately modernised and with continued community involvement, patronage increased by 25 per cent between 1984 and 1986 alone. More economies were deemed necessary though and in May 1991 BR controversially slashed the Whitby service from seven trains each way to just four. The Nunthorpe commuter service was also drastically reduced. Within two years the line's financial performance had improved by 50 per cent and the service remained little changed up to summer 2006, though it is interesting to note that

with five trains each way the Sunday service was superior to that operating on weekdays.

Now the Whitby branch is one of the country's first community railways giving local communities a much greater say in how it is run and for which the Esk Valley Railway Development Company was set up in 2001. Its aims include attracting more passengers by running a more attractive and more frequent service, possible removal of the Battersby reversal, and improved signalling so that NYMR trains can run into Whitby. Already, recent summers have seen regular weekday steam trips between Whitby and Glaisdale and in 2006 a Friday evening music train with a live band and a bar.

Freight traffic

Freight operations in Cleveland have always been geared to its great industries, predominantly steel and chemicals. Inward raw materials like coal, coke, limestone, ore and outgoing products such as steel, fertilizers and bulk liquids have traditionally made up most loads, along with a mix of local traffic incidental to the highly industrial and remote rural communities making up Cleveland.

Nowadays, all freight traffic in Cleveland is concentrated along the Thornaby-Redcar-Boulby corridor but at one time the whole district reverberated to the sound of engines working seemingly endless processions of goods and mineral trains.

Most freight trains in Cleveland were trip workings arranged locally to balance the supply of loads at origin with demand at destination and were not shown in the main working timetable. The only timetabled trains were generally express freights between Newport yards, the south and Tyneside. These were mostly class F and H trains. The winter 1959/60 working timetable showed a total of eight daily trains from Newport to the north via either Ferryhill or the coast and 25 to the south via Northallerton.

The class F(fitted with automatic brake on not less than a fifth of vehicles) and H(not fitted with automatic brake) trains ran to and from such places as Tyne Dock, Addison Yard(Blaydon), Heaton, Consett, Leeds Neville Hill, Whitemoor, Normanton, Mirfield, Healey Mills, Mottram, Dewsnap, Thirsk, Hull, York, Annesley and Woodford Halse. Another 12 ran from the north and 18 from the south. Before Tees Yard opened some trains conveyed traffic to/from the South West which had to be remarshalled at York. Just two class C fully fitted express goods trains ran from Newport and one from Middlesbrough Goods, all to York Dringhouses. There were none inward.

Apart from locally mined iron ore, much was brought in from outside the area. At one time this came from Cumberland via Stainmore but timetabled trains also ran from the East Midlands. The 1959/60 working timetable showed two a day following each other from Storefield quarries with their corresponding return workings departing Newport Foreshore Up Independent; one to "the London Midland Region" and the other to Clay Cross. Three trains a day came from Tyne Dock.

Little in the working timetable there may have been but the number of local trip workings was phenomenal. Listed in the locally-issued Freight and Mineral Trains book, they were given start times, critical intermediate times only, drivers and guards booking-on times and working instructions. The book issued on 5th November 1951 showed 91 trip duties for Newport engines and men every 24 hours; Middlesbrough engines and men had 41 trip duties and the mainly passenger shed at Saltburn one. Another 19 trips from Darlington, Northallerton, West Auckland, Stockton, Haverton Hill and West Hartlepool depots worked into Cleveland making a staggering 152 trip duties(usually involving at least two journeys but often more) every 24 hours on weekdays! Middlesbrough engines and men mostly worked the mineral turns, including local ironstone trafffic, while Newport had the goods as well as mineral traffic and all local trips along the south bank.

Newport trip workings in 1951 plied continuously between all the iron and steel plants, engineering works, factories, depots, docks and goods yards. Thirteen a day went up to Carlin How, often conveying coke and limestone for Skinningrove works and ironstone empties, with 11 returns - the other two returning via Nunthorpe. Others went further afield: to Darlington, St. Helens Auckland and Randolph Colliery, Ferryhill, the Stockton yards, West Hartlepool, various Durham collieries and to Bearpark up on the Durham-Consett line.

Newport trip N28 was a typical local working: driver signs on at 12 noon, guard at 1pm. Light engine from shed to Newport No.1 Down yard and depart at 1.30pm to Tilery(detach and attach wagons by 2.30pm), then to Redcar works(detach), Coatham works(attach by 3.45pm.) To Newport No.1 Up yard (detach wagons) and light engine to No.1 Down yard (attach wagons by 5pm.) To Normanby(detach,) Cargo Fleet Long Roads(attach) and to Newport No.1 Up(detach.) Light engine to Marsh branch(attach wagons by 6.45pm.) Return to Newport yard, detach wagons and light to shed.

Middlesbrough mineral turns went to a range of east, west and north Durham collieries and coking works, to Weardale and Wensleydale for limestone, and with exchange traffic to Thirsk.

In November 1951, there were eight daily local ironstone duties, five worked by Middlesbrough engines and men. M4 trip left Tees works with 25 empties at 4.30am for two return trips between North Skelton mine and Grangetown ore crusher; trip M5 left South Bank at 5am with 25 empties for Lumpsey mine, brought loaded wagons back to the Grangetown crusher, then took another 25 empties from Redcar to Longacres mine, returning loaded to Cleveland ironworks before ending with a trip from Grangetown to Redcar and Tees works. M6 left Tees works at 7.30am to serve Kilton and Lingdale mines, bringing the loads back to Acklam ironworks. M7 left Tees Works at 11.30am and brought ore from North Skelton to the Grangetown crusher, then going from Tees works to Lumpsey or South Skelton mines as required; and M8 left Tees Works at 2pm to work Kilton mine-Grangetown crusher-South Skelton mine and back to Acklam ironworks via Nunthorpe. Of Newport's two ironstone trips, N72, left Newport Klondyke Sidings with empties at 3am for Carlin How where it collected 25 empties and proceeded to South Skelton mine to detach and attach wagons before returning via Nunthorpe to Acklam works. N96 was a general goods which left Newport No.2 Down yard at 9am for Brotton, serving Longacres, North Skelton and Lumpsey mines as required, then continuing to Boosbeck where it detached ore empties and served South Skelton mine as required before returning to Newport via Nunthorpe.

The Saltburn trip also worked ore amongst its

On 10th June 1957, J26 0-6-0 No. 65763 was working a westbound trip past Middlesbrough East signal box and along the goods lines which pass behind the station. The locomotive is displaying a local headlamp code which does not necessarily indicate the class of train. Middlesbrough docks are behind the train along with an LMS-design 2-6-4T while a DMU occupies the carriage sidings on the right. *Neville Stead collection*

varied duties. The rostered J27 loco and brakevan first went to Upleatham sidings, attached wagons and continued to Carlin How where it was instructed to "work the zig-zag and Carlin How goods yard as required." Leaving Carlin How at 12 noon, the engine and brake van again attached wagons at Upleatham before changing crews at Saltburn West. It then returned to Carlin How, shunted as required, leaving at 3.45pm for Brotton where it attached ore from Kilton which it took to Redcar or Cleveland works, or to Grangetown. The engine and van then returned to Upleatham, picked up more wagons for Carlin How where on Mondays and Wednesdays it attached 15 empties for Lingdale mine, leaving them at Brotton before returning to Saltburn shed. On the first Wednesday of each month it took oil cans from Redcar station to Tod Point signal box.

The trip book issued on 1st October 1956 showed 77 Newport turns and 37 Middlesbrough turns; Saltburn still had one and 19 came from the other depots making a total of 134 per 24 hours. A new calling point by this time was Lackenby steelworks where exchange sidings known as 'The Grids' controlled by two internal signal boxes had been installed and connected by a flyover to the goods lines on the north side of the Saltburn line at Beam Mill Junction. The number of local ironstone duties

had reduced to five and Longacres mine had closed. Three Middlesbrough ironstone turns remained: M4, M6, and M7. M6 now brought the ore back to Cleveland works. M7, specified a Class 4MT loco, served Kilton and Lingdale mines and brought the ore back to Acklam works, or to Newport yard if it was destined for Consett. Newport's N74, departing with a double load for Carlin How at 8.50am and requiring an assisting engine from Upleatham, took 25 ore empties from Carlin How to North Skelton and from there took ore to Grangetown. N96 worked in similar pattern as before but returned via Saltburn instead of Nunthorpe.

Local pick-up trains served the various wayside yards and coal depots along all the branches until most local depots closed in the 1960s. The October 1956 book shows Redcar, Saltburn and Loftus being served by N82 trip, a class H goods which left Foreshore sidings at 6.15am calling at Redcar, Marske Aero Sidings, Saltburn, Huntcliffe and Carlin How. An instruction read: "Conveys traffic for Redcar, Marske, Saltburn, Skinningrove and stations between Loftus and Whitby. Positions traffic at Redcar as required. Conveys water cans from Longbeck signal box to Marske daily." Beyond Carlin How, the Whitby line was served by a three days a week pick-up which left Whitby in the morning and

On 21st May 1959, J26 0-6-0 No. 65762 heads a load of ironstone from Kilton mine past Lingdale Junction with the branch to Lingdale mine curving away on the right. Interestingly, the loco is carrying no headlamps, just the chalked inscription "Loftus-Kilton." *Peter Cookson collection*

returned in the early afternoon. N73 trip, the 6am Newport-Carlin How double load goods was instructed to "convey Loftus Shed wagons next to the engine." N84 trip served the former Eston branch six days a week, leaving Foreshore sidings at 11am and shunting Eston Goods, Bell's Siding and Flatts Lane, plus Normanby and Ormesby brickworks as required. N85 trip did the Darlington line as far as Urlay Nook. The Guisborough pick-up was listed in the working timetable while N96 served stations from Brotton to Boosbeck as required. A pick-up came from Northallerton(dep 7.30am) to Newport and was instructed: "From Newport conveys traffic for stations Trenholme Bar to Whitby, marshalled in station order next to the engine to be detached at Eaglescliffe." These connected with the Whitby-Eaglescliffe pick-up, a Whitby working shown in the York District September 1955 local working book to leave Whitby at 8.45am and call all stations as required via Grosmont, Glaisdale, Battersby and Stokesley, running non-stop from there to Eaglescliffe and likewise back to Trenholme Bar on the return. One other Esk Valley freight was the 9.30am cattle from Danby calling also at Grosmont and Ruswarp which ran on Wednesdays when required. The Grosmont-Whitby section also saw the 7.45am Malton-Whitby pick-up and its return working which besides shunting at Grosmont,

Sleights, Ruswarp, Whitby and Whitby gas works, was instructed to wait at Woodlands Siding for milk traffic. Another goods ran from Malton to Ruswarp on Mondays and Wednesdays when required, returning as a class H cattle train.

From 1958 all trip duties originating in Cleveland were worked by Thornaby depot which had replaced Newport and Middlesbrough while Saltburn had closed due to dieselisation. The working book issued on 28th November 1960 showed Thornaby with 133 trip duties. Another 12 reached the locality from Darlington, West Auckland, West Hartlepool and Northallerton depots making a total of 145 per 24 hours. Two trips a day now ran to Spennymoor trading estate.

Cleveland ironstone duties remained at five in 1960. T79, engine off shed at 8.30am, brought ore from Lingdale mine to Grangetown; T85, off Tees Works at 6.15am, made two trips between North Skelton mine and Grangetown but would work "other Cleveland mine as required." T86, off Tees Works at 7am, brought ore from Kilton mine to Grangetown, and T101, off Tees Works at 1.30pm, brought ore from Lingdale mine. T96, now the Guisborough pick-up, left Foreshore sidings at 9.45am, travelled outward via Nunthorpe, detached Kilton and Lingdale wagons at Brotton and served North Skelton mine as required before returning via

Saltburn. South Skelton mine had closed, Lumpsey had been incorporated in North Skelton and the iron-stone trips would soon be extinct along with the mines. North Skelton was the last to go, in 1964, by which time all local goods traffic on the lines around Guisborough, Boosbeck, and Loftus had ended.

The Whitby pick-up became Thornaby turn T94 leaving Foreshore at 7.45am and calling all stations from Battersby onwards as required. It served Sleights, Whitby and Castleton Monday to Friday but only shunted Danby, Grosmont, Woodlands Siding and Ruswarp on Mondays, Wednesdays and Fridays and the other yards on Tuesdays and Thursdays. Commercial goods traffic between Picton and Stokesley ceased in 1958, Stokesley then being served by T99 trip. Leaving Foreshore at 5.45am it shunted Sadlers works, Toll Bar sidings, St. Luke's Hospital siding, Ormesby, Nunthorpe, Great Ayton, Battersby and Stokesley. At Battersby it detached Whitby traffic for collection by T94. T99 could be heavily loaded between Newport and Nunthorpe and sometimes had to be split at Middlesbrough Dock Hill sidings, in which case the engine and van had to go back from Nunthorpe to collect the second load. Goods traffic to Stokesley ceased in 1965 but the Whitby trip soldiered on until 1983 when BR stopped serving all remaining small coal merchants, mainly in order to eliminate unbraked 16-ton mineral wagons. One other pick-up surviving the 1960s was the working via Redcar to Carlin How which served coal merchants at Redcar Central and Brotton until 1980.

In 1963 all marshalling in the area was concentrated on the new Tees Yard and trip workings to and from other yards, such as Stockton, ceased or were drastically scaled down. Line closures and the shift towards bulk trainloads between private sidings or terminals further reduced the need for local trips.

The 1970s and early 1980s brought huge changes to the way BR handled freight traffic and Teesside was at the very heart of these changes which were driven by economic recession, the restructuring of Teesside steel manufacturing, and the elimination of unbraked wagonload traffic and hump shunting. Rationalisation of the steel industry across the country led to an increase in interworks movements with Lackenby supplying steel to other plants like Corby,

Leaving Grosmont on 1st April 1961 with Thornaby trip 94, the Whitby pick-up, and returning to Newport No.1 Up yard is Q6 0-8-0 No. 63447. The connection into the bushes on the left leads from the former Grosmont iron-works 'through line' which was shown on a 1942 LNER drawing as serving Hodsman's slag crushing works. Camping coaches are stabled in Grosmont goods yard beyond the back of the train. *Ken Hoole/N. Stead colln.*

Workington and Hartlepool which had ceased making their own. By 1985, BR was moving 250,000 tonnes of blooms a year to Shelton, 225,000 tonnes to Workington, 150,000 tonnes to Skinningrove and 450,000 tonnes of rolled coil to Corby. Redcar ore import terminal and its deep water berth opened in 1974 and quickly grew in importance. From the start, ore was sent to Consett works in up to eight 900-ton trains a day hauled by pairs of Class 37 diesels; bulk ore trains also ran to Workington and Hartlepool. With Redcar furnaces fed by conveyor, main line ore traffic ceased upon the end of iron smelting at these other plants though British Steel continued to move ore along its internal railway to Cleveland furnaces. In the 21st century, all rail traffic from Redcar terminal is imported coal to power stations and other industrial users.

The 1970s also saw the start of potash and rock salt from the Cleveland Potash mine at Boulby along the reinstated portion of the Whitby line. It was predicted that the Boulby output would top a million tons a year for 15-20 years, most of it going to ICI at Billingham. However, traffic consisted mainly of loads from Boulby to Teesport for shipping and to Middlesbrough goods yard for onward distribution. By 1988, the mine was forwarding 768,000 tonnes a year by rail, below the predicted million but in 2007 it is still very much in business after 33 years. On

the down side, the Shell oil refinery at Teesport, opened in 1968, closed in 1985 after a short spell being supplied with hot semi-refined oil brought from Stanlow, Cheshire, by a 2,000-tonne train, the heaviest to regularly cross the Pennines. ICI's Wilton power station was converted to coal firing in 1988, being served by two trains a day from Butterwell opencast in Northumberland. More business came to the Wilton branch the following year when a new Freightliner terminal was opened in the ICI estate, replacing the original one at Stockton.

By summer 1986, the number of local trips working off Thornaby was just 27 per 24 hours. The total number of freights in the summer 1989 working timetable consisted of 20 to the south and 18 return, and 10 to the north with 14 return. They included fully air-braked Speedlink express services to and from such places as Dundee, Stranraer, Ayr, Haverton Hill, Willesden, Parkeston Quay, Eastleigh, Stoke Gifford, Bescot and Warrington, catering for remaining wagonload traffic which at that time was still considerable. Block trains ran direct between Lackenby steelworks and dedicated terminals such as Wakefield and Wolverhampton or other steelworks without marshalling at Tees Yard where they might stop only to change crews or for staging. Limestone trains for Redcar furnace came from both Wensleydale and Shap. Freightliner

Traffic from the new Cleveland Potash mine at Boulby came on stream in May 1974 and built up steadily from then on. On 7th September 1993 with the Cleveland Way footpath on the left, English Electric Type 3 No. 37415 *Mt. Etna* and its load of potash cling to the edge of Hunt Cliff between Carlin How and Brotton.
Stephen Chapman

The Whorlton Mines branch had closed by the late 19th century but the layout at Potto required a stub to be retained as a headshunt for access to the goods yard on the left This view taken from the bridge carrying Goulton Lane over the branch shows G5 0-4-4T No. 67278, from 51E Stockton shed, leaving the station with a Stockton to Whitby train some time before the service was withdrawn in 1954. *J.W. Armstrong Trust*

services operated between Wilton and Southampton, Stratford, Felixstowe and Trafford Park. Speedlink services were abolished in the early 1990s but many of the block trains still run in 2007.

All change

Economic boom, depression, nationalisation, rationalisation, modernisation, privatisation - they've all been a constant cause of change to Cleveland's railways right from the start and it's still going on today.

The iron mines, inland iron works and associated railways were early casualties. Ironstone branches would close as their mines became uneconomic or worked out; some new ones opened to serve new mines but generally their numbers declined steadily from the 1870s to the 1960s as reserves dwindled. Although Cleveland ironstone was a major source of home-produced ore, it was not best quality and had to be mixed with ore imported or brought from other parts of England. As imports gradually replaced local ore, the iron and steel industry became totally concentrated along the south bank of the Tees, nearer to both its supplies and its markets.

One of the first railways to go was the Codhill mines branch - in the early 1870s when the inland iron industry was still very active. The Whorlton mines branch from Potto had closed by the late 19th Century and the Chaloner branch had been lifted by 1914. During the 1920s, the Port Mulgrave tramway and jetty were replaced by an incline leading up to main line sidings at the Boulby end but it too was subsequently abandoned as the mines became uneconomic. The Rosedale railway is reputed to have shifted nearly 10 million tons of iron ore during its time, most of it in the 19th century. Production declined rapidly after the 1870s and ceased altogether at the end of 1925. The removal of calcining dust continued until 1928 when the whole system was closed. By then just about the only surviving ironstone branches were around Skelton, Lingdale and Eston. With no chance of redevelopment on the moors, traces of the Rosedale railway survive in the 21st century.

It was a different story along the south bank. Prior to the first world war, industry grew so fast that the railway struggled to cope with all the goods traffic. To meet this challenge, Newport marshalling yards

25

Hinderwell(for Runswick Bay) station had probably never been so busy outside the summer holiday season as it was on Saturday 3rd May 1958. Many of these passengers had come a long way to travel on the 4.27pm Scarborough-Middlesbrough behind Middlesbrough shed's well-polished L1 2-6-4T No. 67754. It was the last train and there would be no more - ever. *I. Davidson/Colour-Rail 1617*

were extended towards Thornaby with the addition of Erimus hump yards in 1908 and for a second time the passenger lines were diverted inland. Then in 1916 the NER - always a leader in railway technology - completed electrification on the 1500 volt dc overhead wires system of the Newport-Shildon line which fed the Teesside steel industry with most of its coal and limestone. It was operated by ten Bo-Bo locomotives, one of which is pictured during BR days in Railway Memories No.17.

Economic decline after the first world war culminated in the Great Depression of the early 1930s which brought a massive drop in traffic as many businesses shrank or folded altogether. It came just as the efficiency of the Newport-Shildon operation was being called into question and with the infrastructure due for renewal, the London & North Eastern Railway - which succeeded the NER in 1923 - ceased electric operation on 1st January 1935 and returned the line to steam power. Besides this, Newport Down Goods yard was closed in 1931, the remaining Newport and Erimus yards substantially reduced in 1936 and the Erimus name dropped. More of the system was lost when the mines branches to Spawood, Stanghow and Skelton Park were closed in 1932, c1934 and 1938 respectively. The second world war brought an upturn in goods traffic and Newport yards

were busy again while the post-war manufacturing drive kept them going through the 1950s.

Nationalisation and the creation of British Railways in 1948 brought a rash of closures over a decade before Beeching took the reigns. First to go was the Grosmont-Beckhole branch which had hung on by delivering goods and coal to Esk Valley cottages because there was no road. A road was laid in 1951 and this survivor of the original Whitby & Pickering Railway was redundant. Balanced against this, a goods branch opened in the same year to ICI's chemicals plant at Wilton.

A more serious closure took place on 14th June 1954 when passenger services between Picton and Battersby were withdrawn. Goods traffic on the Picton-Stokesley section ceased from 1st December 1958, and that section closed completely, the track from Picton to Trenholme Bar being used for wagon storage for some time afterwards.

The biggest closure took effect on 5th May 1958 when the cliff top line from Loftus to Whitby West Cliff was shut completely, BR claiming it could not justify the cost of maintaining five substantial viaducts when the line was barely used for nine months of the year. The Skinningrove zig-zag was also abandoned in 1958.

At this time, Newport yards were being converted

into a big modern marshalling yard. Tees Yard, which incorporated the latest fully automated hump shunting methods capable of handling 7,500 wagons a day, was one of four major new marshalling yards-being built in the North Eastern Region to replace numerous small, widely scattered and outdated yards. It included a brand new motive power depot and although designed to become a diesel depot, Thornaby depot included all steam facilities such as a mechanical coaling plant which could coal four locomotives at a time and a modern roundhouse. Not only did it replace Newport and Middlesbrough sheds, but ultimately Stockton and Haverton Hill too. To make room for the yard and depot, the passenger lines were diverted to the south for a third time. The development included colour light signalling and route relay interlocking controlled from a new power signal box which replaced all intermediate mechanical boxes between Bowesfield and Middlesbrough West. Thornaby depot opened in 1958 while Tees Yard was officially opened in May 1963 after being phased in over several years. But, with the traffic for which it was built already declining, the yard never fulfilled its potential and has contracted steadily ever since.

Another significant development in 1963 was the opening of Tees Dock, three and a half miles nearer to the sea than Middlesbrough, 17 years after the Tees Conservancy Commission had been authorized by Parliament to build it. It has since become the main rail-served port on Teesside. Middlesbrough was in decline during the 1950s despite investment in new cranes and transit sheds. In the age of the lorry, poor road access became a serious handicap with many cargoes having to be moved in internal rail wagons between ship and a point where they could be transferred to or from lorries. In the 1970s £5 million worth of expenditure was needed to keep the dock functioning but with it handling little over two per cent of the total traffic of the Tees & Hartlepool Port Authority which had taken it over from the British Transport Docks Board in 1967, the cost could not be justified. Middlesbrough Dock closed on 31st July 1980 and much has since been filled in and redeveloped - Middlesbrough football club's new Riverside stadium occupying part of the site.

With Guisborough-Loftus passenger trains axed on 2nd May 1960, the Guisborough-Boosbeck section was shown in the 1960 Sectional Appendix as 'temporarily closed.' Loftus closed to goods on 12th August 1963 and the line was cut back to Skinningrove steelworks, enabling the removal of a tight bridge over the A174 road. The early 1960s saw

During the transition from Newport yards to Tees marshalling yard, Q6 0-8-0 No. 63355 passes Thornaby motive power depot with a westbound trip on 9th February 1962. On the left, the ground has been cleared for the new Up Staging Departure sidings. Three quarters of the track used for Tees Yard was recovered from closed lines elsewhere. *Peter Rose*

off the ironstone branches to Kilton and Lingdale upon closure of the mines. With North Skelton mine closing in January 1964, Guisborough to passengers in March and to goods in August, and Boosbeck to goods in September, the curtain came down on all the lines linking Nunthorpe with Guisborough, Boosbeck, Lingdale, Brotton and North Skelton.

Goods trains were withdrawn from the Whitby-Scarborough and Pickering lines in 1964 as a prelude to the biggest blow yet to hit Whitby. Despite sustained opposition, the complete closure of the lines between Bog Hall Junction, Prospect Hill Junction and Scarborough, and withdrawal of passenger services between Whitby and Malton together with complete closure of the line between Grosmont and Pickering, went ahead on 8th March 1965. A section of the Scarborough line was retained across Larpool Viaduct to Hawsker in the hope of traffic from a projected potash mine but this failed to materialise and the track was lifted in 1973. August 1965 saw the Battersby-Stokesley section closed completely, the old Cleveland Railway between Cargo Fleet and Normanby in October 1966, and the Saltburn West-Crag Hall line reduced to single track around the same time.

Potash did materialise at Boulby where Europe's deepest mine was sunk to bring it out of the earth for use in the chemical and fertilizer industries. In what was a major boost for Cleveland's railways, the old Whitby line from Skinningrove to Boulby was relaid complete with a new viaduct over the A174, and

opened on 1st April 1974. Double track was restored between Saltburn West and a point near Skelton Beck viaduct. Traffic built up and the line down to Saltburn West came alive again with trains of potash and salt as well as those still serving the steelworks.

The steel industry underwent continual rationalisation after the second world war with a steady shift from the old works around Middlesbrough to bigger, more modern plants further east. Following nationalization and the creation of the British Steel Corporation, duplication amongst the various Teesside works was steadily eradicated. The process reached its climax in the late 1970s when the plants at Redcar and Lackenby were transformed into a big new, fully integrated Teesside works. This included the new Redcar blast furnace - Europe's biggest - close to the river where it could be directly fed imported ore brought in by ship, and adjacent coke ovens which since the virtual elimination of Britain's coal mining industry have also relied on coal from ships. The Lackenby steel plant was enlarged and modernised and the two portions linked by the double track 'hot metal railway' for carrying molten iron from the furnace in specially insulated 'torpedo' wagons. To accommodate this development, the Middlesbrough-Redcar main line had to be moved onto a new alignment further south. British Steel's private station, Warrenby halt, was replaced by a new one on the new alignment called British Steel Redcar which was directly linked to new offices. The

On the stretch of Middlesbrough-Redcar line which had to make way for the new Teesside iron and steel complex, English Electric Type 3 No. 37002 passes a dilapidated Warrenby halt with a Skinningrove to Tees Yard freight at 5.2pm on 16th June 1978. Two days later trains would be using the new alignment with a new halt at British Steel Redcar. *David Holmes*

new line and station were opened on 19th June 1978.

As a result of these changes and the damaging economic recession of the early 1980s, other steelworks were steadily closed until only Cleveland furnaces, Skinningrove mills and South Bank coke ovens remained besides the Lackenby/Redcar complex. Cleveland furnaces closed in 1993.

During this time, Tees Yard shrunk dramatically, the Down yard being totally abandoned. Only two main groups of sidings, one for Up departures and Down arrivals(on the north flank of Thornaby traction depot) and the truncated former Up yard for sorting and wagon stabling remain in use along with four roads of the Down reception sidings for staging. Other remaining sidings are stuffed with stored wagons and locomotives while near-Amazonian undergrowth is steadily partitioning various sections of the yard from each other.

Even with the added potash traffic there was scope for the lines east of Middlesbrough to be slimmed down in the late 1980s while Cargo Fleet and Grangetown stations were closed in 1990 and 1991 respectively. To meet new development, South Bank station was moved 700 yards further east in July 1984 and a new halt opened at Longbeck, between Redcar East and Marske, in May 1985.

Bit by bit, the Whitby line was rationalized in the 1980s and 1990s. Whitby, Bog Hall and Sleights signal boxes were closed in 1984 following the end of goods traffic, the Whitby-Sleights section singled, Whitby goods yard abandoned and the station reduced to just one active platform. In 1986 the Middlesbrough-Nunthorpe section was singled leaving a passing loop at Nunthorpe. This was followed in the early 1990s by a "No Signalman Token" signalling system. The remaining signal boxes were abolished except for Nunthorpe which supervised the whole line. Beyond Nunthorpe, the line was divided into three token sections: to Battersby, Battersby-Glaisdale and Glaisdale-Whitby, drivers exchanging tokens in lockers provided at Battersby, Glaisdale and Whitby "remote token stations."

In 2007, despite a massive rundown in industry and all the line closures and cutbacks over the years, Cleveland still has plenty to interest transport and engineering enthusiasts, whether it be freight operations at Tees Yard, locomotives at Thornaby depot, the busy industrial railways of Teesside steelworks and its awesome blast furnace, or other delights like the Middlesbrough transporter bridge and the seals in the now much cleaner river. Saltburn has its genuine water-balance cliff railway, a miniature railway, the fine selection of classic tractors used by fishermen for towing their boats to the sea, and a breathtaking walk along the Cleveland Way to share the cliff edge with the Boulby potash trains. The Esk Valley branch to Whitby is recognised as one of the country's most scenic and the NYMR from Grosmont to Pickering one of the leading steam lines. All around the area are the archaeological remains of railways and industries past, providing a fascinating subject for study in their own right.

The end. A chilling scene at Guisborough in early 1964 with a two-car Metro-Cammell diesel unit being prepared for its return to Middlesbrough just weeks before the service was axed. *Neville Stead collection*

Thornaby station(South Stockton until 1892) looking west on19th May 1958 with Brush Type 2 No. D5510 having brought BR officials and guests to view the new motive power depot.

This island platform station dates from 1882 when the original was replaced to make way for addition of the goods lines on the right. The buildings were demolished and replaced by waiting shelters during the 1980s after the station became unstaffed but a new ticket office, waiting room, refreshment bar and other facilities were provided in 2002. *K. H. Cockerill / J. W. Armstrong Trust*

ALONG THE SOUTH BANK TO SALTBURN

In 1960 the Thornaby-Saltburn passenger lines were signalled by Absolute Block with Permissive Block between Middlesbrough West and East. Signal boxes were: Thornaby East(1647yds from Bowesfield Jn.), Newport East(1 mile 545yds from Thornaby East), Old Town Jn.(818yds), Middlesbrough West(1211yds), Middlesbrough East(326yds), Guisborough Jn. (522yds), Whitehouse (1022yds), Cargo Fleet(871yds), South Bank(1291yds), Eston West (904yds), Grangetown(1m 198yds), Tod Point(1m 1538yds), Fisherman's(1237yds), Redcar (1m 1252yds), Upleatham(1m 793yds), Longbeck(1m 95yds), Marske (618yds), Tofts(1451yds), Saltburn West (979yds) and Saltburn(842yds.) Signalling on goods lines was Permissive Block with no block on some sections. Signal boxes controlling goods lines only were at Old River and Foreshore(Newport,) Dock Hill (Middlesbrough) and Normanby.

Goods lines(exclusive of Newport yards) were Bowesfield Jn.-Newport East(Up & Down), Newport East-Old Town Jn.(one Up & two Down), Old Town Jn.-Dock Hill(Up & Down,) Dock Hill-Guisborough Jn.(one Up & two Down,) Guisborough Jn.-Whitehouse (Up & Down,) Whitehouse-Normanby (one Up & two Down), Normanby-South Bank(one Up & three Down), South Bank-Grangetown(one Up & two Down), Grangetown-Tod Point(one Down), Tofts-Saltburn West(Up & Down.) There was an Up Refuge Siding at Grangetown, Up and Down Goods Loops at Redcar, and an Up Goods Loop at Saltburn West.

By 1969 all goods lines east of Grangetown except the Redcar loops had been abandoned and Fisherman's box replaced by Kirkleatham 1408yds nearer to Redcar. An Appendix supplement dated 4th May 1970 showed Middlesbrough East, Guisborough Jn., Saltburn West and Saltburn signal boxes plus one Normanby-South Bank Down Goods line and the Redcar Up Goods Loop all abolished and signalling made Track Circuit Block between Longbeck and Saltburn West. Kirkleatham and Upleatham boxes were no longer block posts.

Newport engine shed, coded 51B in the Darlington district during BR days, was situated east of the old river between the Up hump yard and the Tees. Being on soft land reclaimed from marshes, the first shed suffered from subsidence only a few years after it was completed in 1881 in spite of extra deep foundations and had to be completely rebuilt. The replacement, consisting of a double roundhouse, was completed in 1890 and lasted until 1st June 1958 when it was superseded by the new Thornaby depot after which the site was cleared and swallowed up by Tees marshalling yard.

Around one of the roundhouse turntables on 28th September 1957 are, from left: J26 0-6-0 No. 65744, Q6 0-8-0 No. 63371, J26 0-6-0 No. 65740, and J94 0-6-0ST No. 68011. *P.B. Booth/Neville Stead collection*

Locomotives allocated to 51B Newport in January 1957

Q6 0-8-0: 63360/70/1/80/8/9/93/6/63426/30/45/7.
J26 0-6-0: 65730/2/4/6/8/40/41-6/ 9-63/5-70/2/3/4/7/8.
J94 0-6-0ST: 68011/23/49/60/2. T1 4-8-0T: 69911.
WD 2-8-0: 90014/16/27/68/74/6/81/90/1/8/132/230/73/373/409/24/6/34/5/46/
      51/2/7/9/61/2/5/75/81/7/8/500/3/17/603/5/25.
Total: 93

Travelling through the middle of Newport yards from west to east were, on the north side, the Down goods line, No.1 Down Yard reception lines, Thornaby Ironworks signal box (closed 1939) and No.1 Down Hump Yard. On the south side were No.2 Up Hump Yard, its reception lines and the Up goods lines. East of the old river were Old River signal box, a Down goods flat yard, the engine shed, Foreshore signal box and another Down goods flat yard. Immediately south of those were No. 1 Up Hump Yard and its reception lines. The flat yards were known locally as Klondyke and Foreshore.

SHORT MEMORIES

Autumn 1955: Diesel shunters take over hump shunting at Newport yards and the T1 4-8-0T hump locos stored. The diesels must refuel at Darlington.

4.4.59: Whitby's last locos, 2-6-4Ts 42083/4/5 and 2-6-0s 77004/ 77013 transferred away after DMUs take over Malton services.

Whit. Sunday 1960: B16 4-6-0 61412 brings a special to Saltburn.

Whit. Monday 1960: Class 5 4-6-0 45363 (12A) & V2 2-6-2 60819 (64A) visit Saltburn.

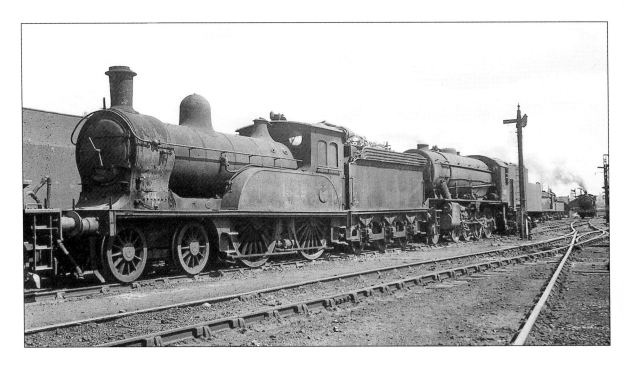

Wartime in Newport shed yard
Above: Class D17/1 4-4-0(NER Class M,) LNER No. 1629, keeps company with the more run-of-the mill
WD 2-8-0s on 6th August 1944. Built in 1893, No. 1629 was officially withdrawn in September 1945.
Neville Stead collection

Below: No. 2317, one of the United States Army Transportation Corps S160 2-8-0s built to the British loading
gauge and shipped over from America to aid the war effort stands face to face with an ex-NER 0-6-0. Working
in Britain for a short time, these engines then followed the allies into Europe after the D-Day invasion.
Neville Stead collection.

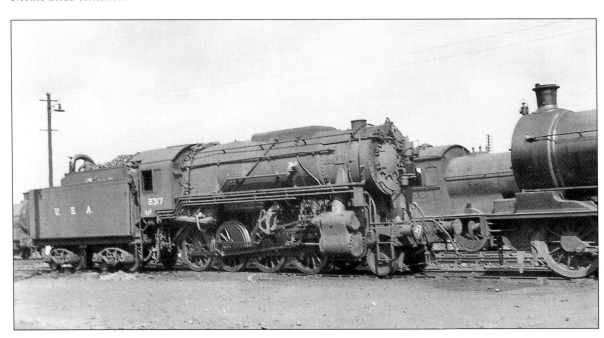

Above: Beneath a battery of NER slotted signals at the west end of Newport No.2 Up Yard (Erimus Up Mineral Yard until the 1930s,) Middlesbrough-based Q6 0-8-0 No. 63375 has charge of westbound mineral empties while J94 0-6-0ST No. 68037 stands alongside. The passenger lines to Middlesbrough are in the foreground and the slag bank of the old Thornaby ironworks on the far left. *Peter Cookson collection*

Below: Commissioned on 1st June 1958, the all-new Thornaby motive power depot, coded 51L, was built with diesels in mind but it would have to be a fully-fledged steam shed for another six and a half years.
Here, in 1959, J26 0-6-0 No. 65730 and Q6 0-8-0 No. 63364 rest inside the straight shed. The concrete beam structure was standard in the 1950s and widely used for modernising other North Eastern Region locomotive sheds. *Neville Stead collection*

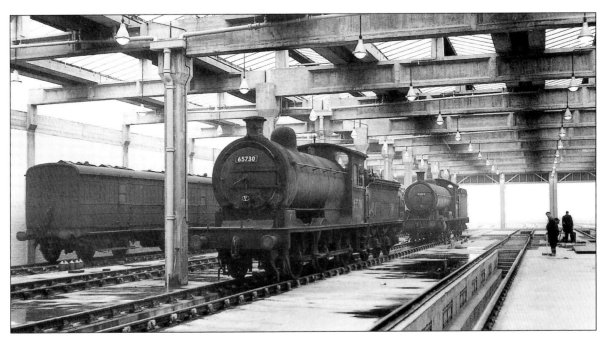

Above: Among diesel types associated with Thornaby depot during the early 1960s were the Clayton Type 1s and D8591 is seen in the roundhouse alongside another member of this short-lived class on 9th August 1964. Thornaby became a diesel depot when it closed to steam in December 1964 and remains an important English Welsh & Scottish Railway loco depot in 2007. The octagonal roundhouse had a 70ft open air turntable with 22 covered stalls. It was demolished in 1988, although the east wall survived and the turntable pit can still be seen from passing trains. There was another 70ft turntable out in the yard.
N.W. Skinner/J.W. Armstrong Trust

Below: Thornaby depot layout at the time of opening in 1958.

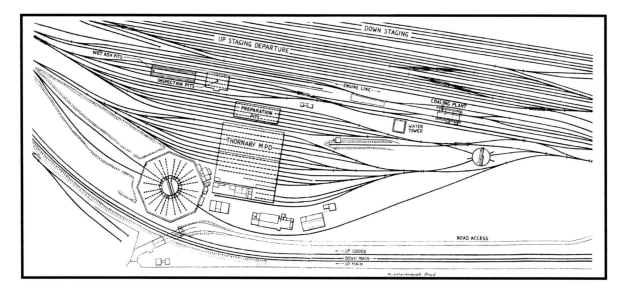

Above: With the roundhouse behind them, J72 0-6-0T No. 69016 and J26 No. 65755 stand outside the straight shed on 25th March 1962. *Robert Anderson*

Below: A line-up of seven 0-6-0 tank engines rest from their various pilot duties with the straight shed on the right and the four-road preparation shed on the left; J72 No. 68684 leads and a J94 stands at the far end on 19th July 1959. In 1960, Thornaby shed provided shunting engines for 29 pilot duties covering work at the various yards and docks. *David Holmes*

Above: More Thornaby 0-6-0 tank engines outside the shed on 19th July 1959. J71 No. 68272 is on the left while J77 No. 68406, its rounded cab branding it as a product of York Queen Street Works, is centre and a J94 0-6-0ST is in the shadows on the right. No. 68406 was withdrawn just four months later. *David Holmes*

Below: It's amazing to think that the age difference between J72 0-6-0T No.69002 and English Electric Type 4 diesel No. D247 was only 10 years, the J72 being one of a batch of these 1898-design locos built by BR at Darlington Works between 1949 and 1951. Here, 69002 shunts departmental wagon DE214193 in Thornaby shed yard on 9th February 1962 as a genuinely elderly J26 0-6-0 shuffles off shed in the right distance. *Peter Rose.*

Above: The W. Worsdell J26 0-6-0s(NER Class P2 introduced in 1904) were the workhorses of Teesside and by summer 1961 all but two of the surviving 20 locos were allocated to Thornaby where they worked out their final days until the last seven were withdrawn in June 1962. At least nine workstained former NER 0-6-0s, mostly J26 with No. 65778 nearest, simmer in Thornaby shed yard at 6.40pm on 29th May 1960. *David Holmes*

Right: At 3.45pm on 19th July 1959, Thornaby's only J25 0-6-0, No. 65720, stands outside the shed with J71 0-6-0T No. 68272 and Ivatt Class 4 2-6-0 No. 43072. No. 65720 had migrated from Middlesbrough where it was the shed's only surviving member of the class, having previously been at Northallerton.
David Holmes

Locomotives allocated to 51L Thornaby, July 1962

Ivatt Class 4 2-6-0: 43015/57/70/5/101; V2 2-6-2: 60806/46/59/85/901/16/46; B1 4-6-0: 61034 *Chiru*/1173/1218/20/57/9; K1 2-6-0: 62001; Q6 0-8-0: 63349/60/4/7/9/70/1/4/5/88/9/93/6/9/401/5/9/11/6/7/20/4/6/8/30/5/42/5/7/52; J39 0-6-0: 64730/57/8/821; J27 0-6-0: 65790/818/20/55/9/84; V3 2-6-2T: 67635/40; J94 0-6-0ST: 68023/39; J72 0-6-0T: 69007/16; BR Standard Class 4 2-6-0: 76024; BR Standard Class 3 2-6-0: 77001/10; WD 2-8-0: 90022/7/48/72/4/81/6/90/1/8/132/273/377/406/34/46/51/2/9/62/79/500/3/17/93; BR/Gardner 204hp 0-6-0 diesel: D2067/9/77/8/99/107/53/4; Drewry 204hp 0-6-0 diesel: D2306/7/17/20/38; 350hp 0-6-0: D3137-51/873/5/6; BR/Sulzer Type 2: D5112/3/51-5/8-75; Birmingham/Sulzer Type 2: D5370-8; English Electric Type 3: D6769.

Total: 159 *Thornaby had 45-ton steam breakdown crane No. 331156 to cover an area from Easington on the Durham coast to Northallerton, Saltburn and Whitby. It could be summoned to emergencies as far away as Amble, Weardale, Catterick and Redmire and when necessary to the Leeds and Hull divisions.*

Left: Thornaby's 45-ton steam breakdown crane in action during an open day at the depot on 10th September 1972. *Stephen Chapman*

Below: The Up yard as seen from the Down side control tower in March 1988. The English Electric Type 3 is just passing over the old River Tees, by-passed in 1810 by the Mandale Cut which considerably shortened the journey for shipping. Originally, Newport yards were left of the old river and Erimus yards to the right. Old River signal box stood just in front of the nearest running lines. *Stephen Chapman*

The 200-acre Tees Yard was officially opened on 21st May 1963 by Dorman Long chairman and managing director Edward T. Judge. It consisted of the Down yard nearest the River Tees which comprised, from west to east: 12 reception roads, 40 main sorting sidings, 6 staging and 8 departure roads plus 10 secondary sorting sidings; and the Up yard comprising from east to west: 12 reception roads, 40 sorting sidings and 12 departure roads. Another 13 sidings were provided for miscellaneous use. Sorting was by gravity, wagons entering each yard over a hump with a 1 in 40 approach gradient followed by a 1 in 16 fall easing through 1 in 66 to 1 in 80. Wagon speeds were controlled by primary and secondary retarders on 1 in 36.9 gradients. The Down yard had a secondary hump on a parallel road which by-passed the primary retarder. Operations were overseen from an elevated control tower overlooking each hump, the Down tower housing the power signal box.

Above: Passing the old Newport station, J26 No. 65757 approaches the yards with an incoming trip from the east bearing a local headlamp code. The station closed in 1915 and never reopened but the platforms were kept for excursion traffic until the 1930s. In 2007 open ground and grazing horses had long ago replaced all the sidings on the left. *Neville. Stead collection*

Below: J26 No. 5734 leaves Newport Down Goods Yard and passes Newport East signal box with an eastbound trip in late LNER or early BR days. This box had two lever frames, one with 49 levers and the other 18 and until 1930 also controlled a level crossing to Samuelson's works, remains of which can just be seen. The box was abolished in August 1962 under stage one commissioning of Tees power box. The overbridge carries the southern approach road to Newport lifting bridge. *Peter Cookson collection*

Above: Dorman Long's Acklam iron works was connected to the Old Town branch by the Acklam Branch which ultimately met the Marsh branch amid the conglomeration of iron and steel plants in this area. Trains loaded with ironstone came straight here from mines in the Cleveland Hills. Among the fleet of locomotives which shunted internally at the works was Barclay 0-4-0ST No. 37, seen here on 16th March 1952.

Below: This Barclay 0-4-0 crane tank, pictured on the same day, was also part of the Acklam Works fleet. *Both Neville Stead collection*

In 1960, the 545-yard branch from Old Town Jn. to Middlesbrough goods yard consisted of five running lines, Up and Down with one extra Down and two extra Up lines. There was no block signalling but besides Old Town Junction there was a signal box at the goods yard. Maximum speed on the branch was 20mph. The single line Acklam branch was worked under One Engine in Steam regulations with a maximum speed of 15mph. By 1969 the Acklam branch no longer featured in the Appendix while the Old Town branch was reduced to two lines controlled by Tees box. The only reference to the Marsh branch gave instructions regarding the operation of two-aspect signals protecting a level crossing giving access to Dorman Long's Britannia and Bridge Construction Works.

Above: The iron and steel plants that once occupied the so-called 'Ironmasters' District' between Newport and Old Town teemed with industrial locomotives of all kinds. Here, at Gjers Mills & Co., is 0-4-0ST *Ayresome No. 8* built by Manning Wardle of Leeds in 1898, works No. 1390.

Below: At the end of the Old Town branch, lines crossed Vulcan Street to various riverside wharves, some of which had small industrial engines of their own. This was 0-4-0ST No. 2, Chapman & Furneaux 1212/1901 at Roddam Dent & Sons Ltd., otherwise known as Dent's Wharf, on 20th June 1951. In 2007 this is the last remaining rail-connected riverside wharf.
Both Neville Stead collection

Above: Looking west from Middlesbrough station on 3rd August 1957. B16 4-6-0 No. 61478 of Starbeck shed passes Middlesbrough West signal box with an arriving express, probably the 9.17 from Leeds City via Ripon. Neck and neck on the goods lines, is J26 No. 65755 bearing the local headlamp code for a working to Lackenby steelworks. Note the Sussex Street crossing keeper's cabin opposite the signal box. Nowadays Middlesbrough West, renamed Middlesbrough and modernised in 1978, controls all movements through the station. The level crossing has since been abolished. *Neville Stead collection*

Left: Looking east on 21st February 1953. The magnificence of the station's original arched roof can still be appreciated even though it was mostly destroyed by a German air raid on 3rd August, 1942. The concrete awnings that will replace it are already in place, extending under the original roof which dated from 1877. That was the same year as York which also suffered enemy action in summer 1942 but thankfully survived.
J.W Armstrong colln.

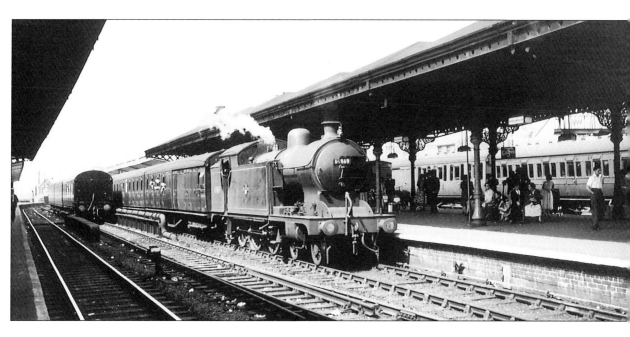

Above: Middlesbrough station on 3rd August 1957. A Darlington-Saltburn train arrives behind A8 4-6-2T No. 69869 of Saltburn shed. The original ironwork canopy support columns survive at the east end of the station in 2007 but the centre road between the platforms has long since been removed. *N. Stead collection*

Below: At 3.15pm on 16th April 1958, Whitby's BR Standard Class 4 2-6-4T No. 80117 awaits departure from platform 3 with the 4.20pm to Scarborough via Guisborough. In less than three weeks, this service will have been withdrawn and diesels will have replaced steam on other local services. The track has since been removed from this bay and the platform fenced off but two of the goods lines on which the J26 is working a Lackenby trip are still in use. *David Holmes*

Above: This 1957 scene shows L1 2-6-4T No. 67754 wearing a 51D Middlesbrough shedplate and looking to be ex-works while preparing to leave platform 3 with a Whitby service. Behind A8 No. 69877, from 50B Leeds Neville Hill, is Dock Hill signal box which controlled only the goods lines. *R. Payne / J.W. Armstrong Trust*

Below: In December 1997, extra trains were run to Whitby in connection with a visit by the replica of Captain Cook's ship, The Endeavour. They were worked by a train from the other end of the country - former Southern Region narrow-bodied Hastings line diesel electric unit No. 1001, strengthened to five vehicles with the addition of a loco-hauled coach. The set stands in platform one forming the 15.40 to Whitby on 12th December. *Stephen Chapman*

Above: Against a backdrop of dockyard cranes, apple green V3 2-6-2T No. 67684 is turned at Middlesbrough shed. *B.G. Tweed / Peter Cookson collection.*

The three roundhouses making up Middlesbrough motive power depot were built between 1866 and 1872. In its later years, the depot became increasingly derelict, until closure took effect on 1st June 1958 when its locomotives and men were transferred to Thornaby. Coded 51D by BR, Middlesbrough shed's workload consisted mainly of passenger and mineral duties.

Below: In the same location as above, J71 0-6-0T No. 68260 keeps company with Q6 0-8-0s in the demolished remains of one of Middlesbrough shed's three roundhouses in July 1956. *I. Davidson / Colour-Rail BRE1611*

Above: Also in 1956, engines in one of Middlesbrough's roundhouses were, from left: push-pull fitted G5 0-4-4T No. 67281, Ivatt 2-6-0 No. 43073, V1 2-6-2T No. 67663, Q6 0-8-0 No. 63340 and V3 2-6-2T No. 67685. Smoke hoods with tall vertical flues were once positioned above the front end of each stall. *E.E. Smith / N.E. Stead colln.*

SHORT MEMORIES

3.5.58: L1 2-6-4T 67754 works the last north-bound Scarborough-Loftus-Middlesbrough train and Standard 2-6-4T 80116 the last south-bound train.

18.6.60: V2 2-6-2 60967 transferred to Thornaby. 60846 joins it a week later.

19.6.60: A3 Pacific 60082 *Neil Gow*(55A) brings an excursion into Redcar.

Locomotives allocated to 51D Middlesbrough
August 1950

Q5 0-8-0: 63282/3/3328/33; Q6 0-8-0: 63349/51/64/8/9/73/5/80/93/409/11/7/20/42/59; J39 0-6-0: 64821/47; J25 0-6-0: 65687/710/26; J26 0-6-0: 65733/64/71/5/6/9; G5 0-4-4T: 67281/338; V1 2-6-2T: 67638/9/47/73; V3 2-6-2T: 67684/5/6/91; L1 2-6-4T: 67755/9/63/4/5/6; J71 0-6-0T: 68260/303/7/12; J77 0-6-0T: 68409/14/22/5; J72 0-6-0T: 68688/9/90/712/3/21/40/54/9006/19. Total: 64

At closure, 31st May 1958

Ivatt Class 4 2-6-0: 43054/7/71/2/3/102; Q6 0-8-0: 63340/9/55/64/8/9/73/5/401/5/9/11/7/20/4/35/42/52; J25 0-6-0: 65720; J26 0-6-0: 65737/75/6/9; J27 0-6-0: 65870; L1 2-6-4T: 67754/9/64/5/6; J71 0-6-0T: 68245/60/90/312; J72 0-6-0T: 68684/88/9/90/712/21/40/9006/19; J50 0-6-0T: 68908/42/8; A5 4-6-2T: 69830/1/4/42; A8 4-6-2T: 69860/6/9/82/91. Total: 59

In 1956, Middlesbrough shed provided engines for 14 booked pilot duties shunting Middlesbrough Goods, Marsh Branch, Cargo Fleet, the former Owners' Railway in Vulcan St., and five Middlesbrough dock turns.

Above: Across the Saltburn lines from the engine shed, No. 63333, one of Middlesbrough's four Q5 0-8-0s at the time, shunts a mixed rake of mineral wagons alongside the docks during early BR days.The Guisborough lines start to curve away in the foreground at Guisborough Junction. *B.G.Tweed / Peter Cookson collection*

Below: Alluding to the difficulty in reaching the quayside by road vehicle, a 1940s critic described Middlesbrough dock as a puddlehole in a railway yard and this view illustrates the point. In the 1950s, a Middlesbrough J72 0-6-0T scurries about amid the mass of sidings which separated the docksides from the outside world. The wagons are loaded with a fascinating array of steel products. *C.I.K. Field Archive*

Above: Looking west onto the cut connecting Middlesbrough Dock with the river in November 1954 as the tug *Caedmon Cross* prepares to move the freighter *Bendigo* out of the dock area. The North Wharf conveyor for loading coal from rail to ship is on the right. *Both pictures C.I.K.Field Archive*

Below: In 1952, the steam tug *Banbury Cross* brings a freighter into the dock .

Right: Looking weary and workworn yet only four years old, BR-built J72 0-6-0T No. 69019 stands alongside the freighter *City of Agra* with a selection of hopper wagons in 1954.
C.I.K.
Field Archive

Below: This 25th June 1979 view shows Middlesbrough Dock in its final years - short on ships yet with a surprising amount of traffic for this late stage. Ex-BR 204hp 0-6-0 diesel shunter No. 3(BR No. D2023) stands with two wagonloads of crates, illustrating how internal wagons still had to be used for conveying cargo between ships and lorries even though some road improvements had been made. *Adrian Booth*
Around this time, Middlesbrough Dock had a fleet of five diesel locomotives. Besides D2023 they were: No.4(ex-D2024), No.1(ex-D2205), 0-4-0 No. 2(Stephenson & Hawthorn 7925/Drewry 2592 of 1959) and No.5(English Electric Vulcan Foundry 4-wheel hydraulic D908/1964.) The Tees & Hartlepool Port Authority painted most of its locos yellow making a colourful sight alongside its bright blue internal wagons.

Above: Most of the Owners of Middlesbrough Estate Railway was sold to the NER in the 19th century but some small sections remained with the company. One of those was in the engineers' timber yard at Whitehouse, east of the docks which is where 0-4-0ST *Estate No.1*, built by Chapman & Furneaux of Newcastle, works No. 1156 of 1898, was still at work on 20th June 1951. *Neville Stead collection*

Trip freights working east of Newport/Tees yards displayed local headlamp codes. The 1969 Sectional Appendix, still showing steam headlamps besides diesel headcodes, instructed: "When Down trains from west of Tees are working through to points east of Tees the special headlamp code or destination letter must be placed on engines at Tees signal box.

"The special headlamp code or destination letter denote the destination of the trains and do not necessarily indicate classification."

The local headlamp codes(with diesel headcode letter in brackets) were:

Below chimney and centre of buffer beam(K) - *East of Grangetown, Grangetown ore sidings, Lackenby steelworks, Whitby branch.*
Centre and above left hand buffer(M) - *Cargo Fleet Inner Jn. and Eston branch.*
Below chimney and above right hand buffer(A) - *South Bank north side, South Bank coke ovens, Tilery Sidings.*
Centre of buffer beam and above right hand buffer(S) - *South Bank south side, Cleveland steelworks and ironworks, Clay Lane sidings.*
Above left hand buffer(G) - *Cargo Fleet ore sidings, Normanby ironworks sidings.*
Centre of buffer beam(P) - *Whitehouse Cochranes, Whitehouse branch, Cargo Fleet station sidings.*
Above right hand buffer(J) - *Dock Hill, Dock Hill Recepetions, Dock Hill Low Level.*
Below chimney and above left hand buffer(O) - *Old Town, Marsh Branch, Middlesbrough Goods Yard.*

Above: Looking east from near Whitehouse signal box on 6th May 1967. K1 2-6-0 No. 62044 just edges into the scene as BR/Sulzer Type 2 No. D5157, displaying a local headcode, shunts Cochranes Ormesby ironworks. The single line sweeping across from left to right goes to North Ormesby gas works as well as a foundry and an engineering works. In the right distance is the massive Cargo Fleet iron and steel plant whose name could be seen embossed on rails across the country in common with Skinningrove and Dorman Long who also manufactured rails. *Robert Anderson*

Below: Cargo Fleet station looking west in March 1968 with Whitehouse signal box in the distance. The station closed in May 1990 having been stripped of its buildings many years before.
R.B. Coulthard/K.L. Taylor collection/NERA

Sentinel 2, a vertical boilered tank engine, unusually with four-coupled wheels, was found at the Cargo Fleet ironworks on September 29th 1951. It was built by Sentinel of Shrewsbury in 1926, works No. 6154.
Neville Stead collection

The 1960 Sectional Appendix showed the surviving Cargo Fleet-Normanby section of the old Cleveland Railway as 3 miles 1095 yards long from Cargo Fleet Junction to Normanby brickworks. The 1085yds of double track to Cargo Fleet Inner Ground Frame was worked "No Block," the single line from there onwards being operated according to "One Engine in Steam" regulations(only one train allowed on the branch at a time.)

The maximum speed was 25mph including the junction with the branch to Eston coal depot but 10mph over a level crossing situated 1276yds from Cargo Fleet Junction.

A rising gradient began at 1 in 120 from Cargo Fleet, steepening to 1 in 25 before reaching Flatts Lane level crossing which was 2 miles 1300yds from Cargo Fleet Junction.

Flatts Lane crossing gates were left closed and padlocked across the railway, the key being kept by the working foreman at Eston station who accompanied trains to open and close the gates. Post Office telephones with outdoor loud bells were provided at Eston station and Cargo Fleet Inner and it was the Cargo Fleet Inner working foreman's job to advise the Eston foreman when a train was leaving for Flatts Lane.

Notice boards at the entrance to the Eston coal depot line and at Normanby brickworks outlet read: "Drivers must not proceed beyond this point unless authorised by the Eston foreman." Hold-up points were provided to prevent movement from the brickworks line towards the crossing until the foreman had advised the driver that the gates had been closed to road traffic. The guard could then change the points to let the train out.

Although the branch closed in 1966 almost a mile remained in use. The 1969 Sectional Appendix showed the section to Inner Ground Frame unchanged but with a maximum speed of 15mph(reduced to single track with "One Train Working" by 1970.) The remaining 630yds beyond that was classed as a shunting area with a 10mph maximum speed. The 1969 Appendix refers to Skippers Lane level crossing where the gates were kept shut across the track and the guard or shunter had to advise the crossing keeper so that the gates could be opened before any movement over the crossing.

The 1956 Handbook of Stations lists the following sidings on the Normanby branch: Bell's Siding; Cleveland Magnesite & Refractory Co. Ltd. (Normanby and Ormesby brickworks); Middlesbrough Co-operative Society; Normanby public coal and mineral depots.

In 1960, Thornaby 93 trip, a class H goods, was booked to leave Newport Foreshore sidings at 11.5am, to detach wagons at Eston Goods and Bell's Siding, and to attach wagons at Bell's Siding(due 3pm,) Eston Goods and Flatts Lane on the return which terminated at Cargo Fleet Long Roads. It also shunted at Cargo Fleet Inner, Flatts Lane, Ormesby brickworks and Normanby brickworks on the outward run when required.

Left: By the water column at Cochranes works on 6th May 1967 was Hawthorn Leslie 0-4-0ST No. 2729, built 1907.

Centre: At the British Steel Corporation's Teesside Bridge & Engineering works, Cargo Fleet, Sentinel steam loco *Teesside No.5* (9629/57) was kept in reserve to four diesels and had not worked for five years when it was called into action after one of them failed. It had been working for two weeks when photographed on 5th July 1971.
Both Robert Anderson

Bottom: South Bank station looking west in March 1968. Opened in 1882 this station closed in July 1984 when it was replaced by a new halt consisting of two timber platforms 700 yards further east.
South Bank had a goods yard with a one-ton crane and was able to handle goods and live-stock. *R.B. Coulthard / K.L. Taylor collection / NERA*

Above: J26 No. 65730 passes South Bank signal box with a westbound trip displaying local headlamps in the 1950s. Dorman Long's new coke ovens, built on the site of South Bank blast furnaces, are in the centre background and Cleveland iron works in the right background. South Bank box closed in 1982 when the goods lines from Whitehouse were abandoned. The present day station is near to the coke ovens.
E.E. Smith / Neville Stead collection.

Left There were two Eston stations. One at the end of the Normanby branch and the one at South Bank, on the junction with the Eston Mines Railway - the derelict remains of which are seen on 15th February 1953, 68 years after closure. This building dating from the 1860s, was renamed South Bank in 1878 but reverted to Eston in 1882 when the South Bank station on the previous page was opened. It closed in 1885 upon the opening of Eston Grange (later renamed Grangetown.) Clay Lane sidings are beyond the buildings
J.W. Armstrong Trust

Clay Lane Siding - trains from Cleveland iron works: Before a train is allowed to leave Cleveland Iron Works the guard must obtain permission from the inspector or person in charge at Clay Lane. The telephone, which is situated in Messrs. Dorman Long & Co.'s box adjacent to the level crossing, may be used for this purpose. Drivers must not proceed until they have a verbal assurance from the guard that the necessary authority has been received. *BR North Eastern. Region Sectional Appendix 1960.*

Above: A rather unusual machine at Cleveland steelworks. In 1958 Dorman Long converted three of its redundant 0-4-0STs to compressed air operation by replacing the boiler with a diesel-powered air compressor, undertaking the work at its own Cleveland workshops. This shot of MC2 (the others were MC1 and MC3) was snatched from a passing train on a very gloomy 9th March 1977.

Below: British Steel 6-wheel diesel electric loco No. 265 *Roseberry*, built by GEC Traction in 1977, works No. 5462, shunts ore wagons near Clay Lane on a remnant of the Eston Mines Railway at Cleveland ironworks on 25th August 1992. The ore has been brought from Redcar import terminal but from 1850 until 1949 it came from the mines. One of the two remaining blast furnaces is on the right but 18 months later they were gone, demolished by explosives. These 27 locomotives are all named after Cleveland ironstone mines except the first, No. 251, which is named after GEC designer Walter Urwin who died before they entered service.

Above: Decrepit signals on the Cleveland ironworks internal railway at the point where the old Eston Mines Railway entered the works. 29th January 1977. *All pictures on this page by Stephen Chapman*

Above: Grangetown station looking east on 2nd February 1970. Lackenby steelworks is on the right while the intersection bridge on the left carries the Beam Mill line which to this day provides the main line connection with the works.

Called Eston Grange when opened in 1885, this station was renamed Grangetown in 1902, presumably to avoid confusion with Eston on the former Cleveland Railway. Grangetown closed on 25th November 1991 but had lost its buildings long before that. *R.B. Coulthard / K.L. Taylor collection / courtesy of K.C. Appleby*

Below: The Beam Mill line connects the main line with Lackenby Grids, three groups of exchange sidings within the works complete with their own steel company signal box. Set up in the 1950s, the grids are the start and finish point for so many of the block steel trains which operate across the British railway network. In the days when most trains still went only as far as Newport Yard for remarshalling, the fireman of Q6 0-8-0 No. 63428 watches for the guard's 'right away' on 9th February 1962. *Peter Rose*

Above: Q6 0-8-0 No. 63389 passes Lackenby with a short class H goods on 9th February 1962.
Peter Rose

The Shell-Mex Teesport refinery(Grangetown) branch was one mile 1025yds long and worked by Electric Token Block controlled entirely by Grangetown signal box with no token provided. Signals for the single line between Grangetown and the refinery exchange sidings were electrically controlled to prevent opposing movements, and to prevent more than one train being on the single line between two stop signals in the same direction of travel at the same time. The maximum speed was 15mph.
The BR Eastern Region(Northern Area)1969 Sectional Appendix stated that only special flame proofed 204hp (Class 03) 0-6-0 diesel shunters Nos. 2046, 2057 and 2093 were allowed to move tank wagons to and from the refinery loading points.

TOD POINT.... A train may be allowed to work along the line between Tod Point signal box and Messrs Dorman Long & Co.'s Warrenby Depots, or Warrenby Sand Sidings, and may return in the wrong direction to the Stop Board lettered: STOP, WHISTLE AND WAIT INSTRUCTIONS at the Warrenby platform end. The driver must be given a wrong line order at Tod Point signal box authorising him to return in the wrong direction.......BR North Eastern Region Sectional Appendix 1960.

Right: Just three days before this line was due to make way for the new Redcar and Lackenby Teesside iron and steel complex, the 16.23 Saltburn-Darlington Metro-Cammell DMU calls at Warrenby halt on 16th June 1978.
David Holmes

Above: Summer Saturdays, bank holidays and race days brought a variety of excursion trains to Redcar, often hauled by more exotic power than the daily diet of 4-6-2 tanks that worked the local services. On 10th June 1957, V2 2-6-2 No. 60915 approaches the resort with a Whit. Monday Sheffield to Saltburn excursion, presumably from Sheffield Victoria as the V2 was a Great Central section engine based at Woodford Halse. Coincidently, 60915 was transferred to Thornaby in September 1959. *Neville Stead collection*

Below: Redcar had a platform on a loop line just west of the main station for handling excursion traffic. This is Redcar Central Special Platform looking east on Whit. Monday 10th June 1957 as an excursion brought in by A5 4-6-2T No. 69834 disgorges its load of day trippers. Stockton-based Ivatt Class 2 2-6-0 No. 46478 waits to clear away the empty stock as A8 No. 69894 departs the main station with what appears to be an additional local train formed of articulated non-corridor stock. *Neville Stead collection*

Above: Virtually brand new from Doncaster Works, BR Standard 4MT 2-6-0 No. 76050 pokes out of Redcar Central trainshed (plain Redcar until 1950) after arriving with an excursion from the west on 21st May 1956. The station was built for just a single track and an Up(westbound) platform was not added untl 1935. In 1970 it reverted to the original platform then in the 1980s the use of two platforms was restored with new buildings provided on the westbound platform in 1988. In the early 1990s the listed trainshed and adjoining buildings were converted into a centre for small businesses and a new eastbound platform built on the centre line just west of the trainshed. *L.A. Strudwick*

Below: It is 1953, horse boxes occupy the loading dock and A8 4-6-2T No. 69891 restarts its Darlington-Saltburn local. Redcar Central had a fairly extensive goods yard capable of handling all types of traffic with warehouses at each end of the station and a five-ton yard crane, and did not close until 6th October 1980. Other depots in the area listed by the 1956 Handbook of Stations were Ings Farm public coal and mineral siding and Kirkleatham Lane depot. The Co-op had a coal siding at Redcar and a private siding served the gas works. The Down goods loop and one siding remain in 2007 while offices occupied by a firm of solicitors have replaced the horse docks. *Neville Stead collection*

Above: With a world war less than two months away, this was possibly one of the last excursions to visit Redcar for some years to come. LNER J39 0-6-0 No. 2695 and ex-Great Central B7 4-6-0 No. 5483 leave Redcar for Saltburn in July 1939. Interestingly, the train number 367 is the same as 60915's on page 56 and, judging by the train engine, is also from Sheffield Victoria. *G. Pierson*

Below: Redcar East Halt was opened in 1929 to cater for new housing in the area, the 'halt' portion of its name later being dropped. It remains open in 2007 though the timber buildings have given way to modern waiting shelters. This is how it looked on 2nd February 1970. *Neville Stead collection*

Above: A8 No. 69878 thunders past Redcar East with a class A Darlington-Saltburn train on 26th June 1954.

Below: BR Standard Class 3 2-6-0 No. 77013 slows its Saltburn-Darlington local for the stop at Redcar East on 19th July 1955. *Both pictures by L. A. Strudwick*

Above: Well polished A8 No. 69866 brings a 1950s Darlington-Saltburn local into Marske station. The goods yard, behind the platform, was listed in the 1956 Stations Handbook as having a one-ton crane and as well as general goods could handle horse boxes and prize cattle vans but only by prior arrangement so far as inwards traffic was concerned. Private sidings were the Green Lane Manure Siding and a War Department Siding. Goods facilities were withdrawn on 5th April 1965. Marske goods shed has been fully renovated and in 2007 remains in private use. *Neville Stead collection*

Below: Marske station looking east on 2nd February 1970. It became unstaffed in 1969 but remains open in 2007, though the buildings have gone and modern waiting shelters grace the platforms. *Neville Stead collection*

Right: Longbeck signal box, 618yds west of Marske station. During simplification of track and signalling in 1969/70, this box had to be retained because of the level crossing. It was therefore re-equipped and took over control of everything east of here, including Saltburn West Jn., Saltburn station and the Crag Hall line. The line to Saltburn West was equipped with Track Circuit Block signalling and the remaining single track into the station worked by Electric Token Block; the Saltburn West-Crag Hall line was reduced to One Train Working, an Annett's key for operating Brotton sidings ground frame being kept at Longbeck box.
K.C. Appleby collection

Centre: Saltburn West signal box in early 1970, just before closure. *Neville Stead collection*

Below: Tofts signal box 1451yds east of Marske station, marked the end of the four-track section from Saltburn West. It closed some time between 1965 and 1969 when the goods lines were removed. This 1950s view shows a filthy A5 4-6-2T passing with a Saltburn-Darlington local composed of the usual articulated stock. *K.C. Appleby collection*

The entrance to Saltburn was marked by the engine shed situated in the 'V' between the station approach and the line climbing away to Crag Hall.
Above: This 1930s view with A5 4-6-2Ts present shows the shed in its original condition with pitched clerestory roof and tall smithy chimney. *J.W. Armstrong Trust.*

Below: The closed shed in what is believed to be August 1962, its roof having been reduced at some time to simple sheet cladding. The two shed roads are rusty but visiting York V2 No. 60968 simmers on the coal yard road. A train stands in the excursion platform in the left distance.
Saltburn shed was coded 51K and almost all its duties were on local passenger trains. It closed completely in January 1958 as Darlington-based diesel multiple units took away its work. Its 4-6-2Ts were dispersed to other sheds in the district to work out their last few months, all the A5s going to Darlington and the A8s to Middlesbrough and West Hartlepool. The shed was later demolished and a house stands on the site in 2007 though the goods shed in the background survives. *T.E.Rounthwaite.*

Above: An impressive array of semaphore signals stands guard over the exit from Saltburn station as A5 4-6-2T No. 69841 awaits departure for Darlington on 21st August 1957.. *L.A. Strudwick*

Below: The new era dawns for Saltburn-Darlington trains. The big Pacific tanks are gone and instead a Metropolitan-Cammell DMU waits in platform one. As at Redcar, the trainshed was single platform style with a hipped and slated overall roof. Nowadays, trains are confined to two bay platforms on the extreme right, the trainshed is gone and a supermarket occupies the whole area left of the nearest bay. *N. Stead collection*

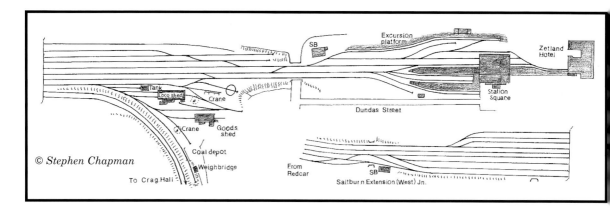

© Stephen Chapman

Excursion platform • SB • Zetland Hotel • Station Square • Dundas Street • Tank • Loco shed • Crane • Crane • Goods shed • Coal depot • Weighbridge • To Crag Hall • From Redcar • SB • Saltburn Extension (West) Jn.

Top: The Saltburn layout as it was c.1913. In 2007 there is just a single line and run-round loop from the junction to the station, two bay platforms and two carriage sidings. *Not to scale*

Left: Saltburn station signal box in early 1970, shortly before abolition.

Below: The track has gone from the excursion platform and the ornate building awaits its fate in this early 1970 view.
Both N. Stead colln.

Top: A depressing view of Saltburn station east end on 2nd February 1970, typical of the post-Beeching years when everything was being stripped to the bare essentials.

Centre: A happier scene in September 1993. The station buildings have been restored and even the N.E. Region tangerine enamel sign still confirms that this is the 'Railway Station.' Like other original buildings in the resort, the hotel and station were made of a white brick from Pease's brickworks in County Durham. *Stephen Chapman*

Bottom: Platform one extended into the formerly railway-owned Zetland Hotel so that guests could step off their train and straight into the hotel. This view was taken in March 1968 and the platform roof is still there in 2007. *Neville Stead collection*

A stop board was positioned about 80 yards from the end of the line and engines needing to run round their trains via the shunting line on the left were the only movements permitted beyond the board without the prior permission of the signalman at the station box.

Above: The first station on the Middlesbrough & Guisborough line, three miles from Middlesbrough, was Ormesby, seen here in August 1961 with L1 2-6-4T No. 67764 arriving from the Middlesbrough direction with a special ordinary passenger working. *Neville Stead collection*

MIDDLESBROUGH-GUISBOROUGH-WHITBY

Below: Ormesby station looking towards Nunthorpe in October 1968. A basic single track passenger halt called Marton now stands here and in 2007 virtually no trace remains of the station shown on this page. The 1 in 40 gradient, which sometimes necessitated the use of banking engines on freight trains, is clearly visible. *Neville Stead collection*

Above: Nunthorpe station in 1968 with a Metro-Cammell DMU leaving for Whitby via Battersby. Semaphore signals still control movements here in 2007. *Neville Stead collection.*

The 1956 Handbook of Stations listed Nunthorpe as having a goods yard equipped with a 2-ton crane.and capable of handling all types of traffic.

Below: It is 1st August 1983 and preserved LMS Jubilee 4-6-0 No. 5690 *Leander* approaches Nunthorpe signal box with a breakdown crane during a transfer movement from the North Yorkshire Moors Railway as the signalman waits for the fireman to hand him the single line token from Battersby. The box has a style of hipped roof commonplace throughout Cleveland. It dates from 1903 but was re-equipped with a smaller 16-lever frame in 1966. *Stephen Chapman*

Above: Nunthorpe station looking towards Middlesbrough in 1968. The low buildings and canopy nearest the camera had been demolished by 1982.
Ken Hoole / Neville Stead collection

Below: Nunthorpe East Junction signal box in 1963 with the Battersby line curving to the right. *G.H. Platt*

The 1960 Sectional Appendix showed the Middlesbrough(Guisborough Jn.) to Crag Hall line worked by Absolute Block signalling with Electric Token on the Crag Hall-Loftus single line. Signal boxes, in the Down direction, were: North Ormesby (673yds from Guisborough Jn.), Pennyman's (1733yds from North Ormesby), Ormesby(1m 508yds), Nunthorpe(1m 1050yds), Nunthorpe East (1m 66yds), Guisborough(3m 1222yds), Boosbeck (3m 363yds), Priestcroft Jn.(668yds), Kiltonthorpe Jn. (1m 1262yds), Brotton (1039yds), Crag Hall(3m 303yds) and Loftus (1m 940yds.) The maximum line speed was 45mph to the junction at Guisborough and 30mph from there onwards. An Up Goods Loop holding 44 wagons, engine & brake van was situated at Pennyman's with a Down Refuge Siding for 35 wagons, engine & van. Nunthorpe had an Up Refuge Siding for 69 wagons, engine & brake van, and Nunthorpe East an Up Refuge Siding for 28 wagons, engine & van. An Up Goods Loop at Boosbeck could hold 52 wagons, engine & brake van. Gradients from Guisborough to Brotton rose at 1 in 100/114.

By 1969 Pennyman's, Ormesby and Nunthorpe East signal boxes had gone along with the loop and refuge siding at Pennyman's and the line speed(to Battersby) had been raised to 50mph.

The 1969 Sectional Appendix also stated that siding points at Nunthorpe were operated by a ground frame released by an Annetts Key kept in the station signal box. The Middlesbrough-Nunthorpe section was singled in 1986, retaining a passing loop at Nunthorpe.

Above: Three miles after Nunthorpe on the line to Guisborough, came Pinchinthorpe station, seen here looking east with the small goods yard just beyond the overbridge. This was the second station, the first also being situated just beyond the bridge. The station closed completely on 29th October 1951. *J.W. Armstrong Trust*

Below: Hutton Gate station in the 1950s with Ivatt Class 4 2-6-0 No. 43072(51D) on a Middlesbrough- Scarborough service. The station was provided exclusively for the use of the Pease family whose estate was at nearby Hutton Hall, but became a public station in 1904 after being disused for three months. It became unstaffed in 1961 and finally closed completely on 2nd March 1964 when the Guisborough service was withdrawn. *N. Stead colln.*

Above: Guisborough Moor looms through the haze as A8 No. 69886 of 50E Scarborough shed enters Guisborough at the head of a Middlesbrough to Whitby local in August 1955. The signal is already 'off' for the train's departure which will involve reversing back to the junction before going forward to Loftus and Whitby. The Cleveland Railway once crossed under this section of line beyond the distant overbridge. The 1955 Working Timetable allowed steam trains 14 minutes in both directions for the 5.5 miles between Hutton Gate and Boosbeck, including station time and reversal at Guisborough. *J.W. Armstrong Trust*

Below: No. 69886 begins its reversal out of the station and past the shed which was once home to one of the Sentinel steam railcars that operated local services in the area between the 1920s and 1940s. After that it housed a G5 0-4-4T oustationed from Middlesbrough until the early 1950s. On the left is the goods shed and the 6 ton yard crane. Guisborough was equipped to handle all types of freight traffic. Passenger services ended on 2nd March 1964 but goods lingered on until 31st August. *J.W. Armstrong Trust*

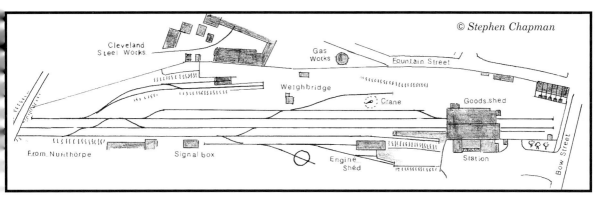

© Stephen Chapman

Above: The layout at Guisborough c.1914 *Not to scale*

Guisborough station weekday departures. Summer 1955

6.38am	6.10am Middlesbrough-Scarborough
8.19am	6.52 Whitby Town-Middlesbrough
	Unadvertised call at Skinningrove
9.34am	9.7am Middlesbrough-Whitby Town
10.39am	8.12am Scarborough-Middlesbrough
11.28am SX	11am Middlesbrough-Whitby West Cliff
	18th July to 19th August inclusive
11.28am SO	11am Middlesbrough-Scarborough
	2nd July to 10th September inclusive
12.41pm SO	Arrival time. 12.15pm from Middlesbrough
12.53pm SO	12.53pm to Middlesbrough
1.34pm	1.7pm Middlesbrough-Whitby Town
	Unadvertised call at Skinningrove on Saturdays
2.12pm	11.43am Scarborough-Middlesbrough
3.28pm SO	1.6pm Scarborough-Middlesbrough
	16th July to 20th August inclusive
4.49pm	4.20pm Middlesbrough-Scarborough
	Unadvertised call at Skinningrove
5.44pm	Arrival time. 5.18pm from Middlesbrough
6.5pm	6.5pm to Middlesbrough
6.27pm SO	4.5pm Scarborough-Middlesbrough
	16th July to 20th August inclusive
7.4pm	4.35pm Scarborough-Middlesbrough
7.34pm SX	6.26pm Whitby West Cliff-Middlesbrough
	18th July to 19th August inclusive
7.52pm	6.33pm Whitby Town to Middlesbrough
10.15pm	8.2pm Scarborough to Stockton(West Hartlepool from 22/8)
	18th June to 10th September inclusive

SHORT MEMORIES

Easter Monday 1961: Jubilee 4-6-0 45566 *Queensland* brings a Saltburn excursion from Bradford. A cracked tender frame is discovered during servicing at Thornaby shed and a B1 4-6-0 takes its return working, 45566 going home light the next day.

Whit. Monday 1961: Jubilees 45569 *Tasmania* (55A,) 45594 *Bhopal*(41C) and Stanier 2-6-0 42977 (5B) all work specials to Saltburn.

7.10.61: Jubilee 45671 *Prince Rupert* (6G) arrives at Middlesbrough with a football special from Liverpool.

The 1960 Sectional Appendix stated that the maximum permitted speed for trains on the 963-yard line between Guisborough station and the junction was 20mph (hauled)and 10mph (propelling.)

Although Guisborough lost all its train services in 1964, one railway remained active in the town until the late 1990s. This was the short standard gauge internal line at Blackett Hutton's foundry situated between Providence Street and the main line. It was used to transfer molten metal between the foundries, employing a 1948-built Ruston & Hornsby 48DS type diesel loco, works No. 265617. Narrow gauge tracks of various gauges also served the casting areas.

The foundry was established in 1861 and especially made plant and equipment for the ironstone mines, including railway items like wheels and track points. It went on to produce all kinds of castings including steel industry plant, marine engineering components, valves and pressure vessels with a reputation for high quality workmanship.

A main line connection was established some time after 1914 and traffic included foundry sand, pig iron and scrap inwards and finished goods outwards.

Above: In the 1950s, BR Standard 4MT 2-6-4T No. 80118 from 50G Whitby shed, waits at the town end of Guisborough station before reversing back to the junction, having arrived from Middlesbrough. After closure, this attractive station was demolished and a health centre built on the site. *E.E. Smith / N. Stead colln.*

Left: On the Cleveland Railway, to the east of Guisborough, Slapewath was once a busy junction where several ironstone mines branches joined the main line. There was nothing much left to see, however, by the time Middlesbrough's V3 2-6-2T No. 67677 passed through with a Scarborough to Middlesbrough train in the mid-1950s. The junction was abolished after closure of the Spa Wood, Stanghow and Skelton Park mines branches in the 1930s. The signal box was still there in the 1950s but switched out. *Ken Hoole / Neville Stead collection*

Right: Boosbeck looking west in the 1950s as an A8 pulls its Middlesbrough train out of the station. About 600 yards further on it will pass South Skelton iron mine on the left. The left hand signal controls entry to the Up Goods Loop. The goods yard on the right had a 5 ton yard crane at the time and was able to handle general goods and livestock for which the cattle dock can be seen. It became an unstaffed public delivery siding when the station closed to passengers on 2nd May 1960 in which guise it stayed open for business until 14th September 1964. *J.W. Armstrong Trust*

Below: The grim scene looking east at Boosbeck in May 1961. The station closed upon withdrawal of the Guisborough-Loftus DMU service and by this time the only booked train on the line was Thornaby trip 96, the Guisborough pick-up, running eastbound only as it returned to Newport yard via Saltburn. *T.E Rounthwaite*

Above: A Scarborough to Middlesbrough train hauled by A8 No. 69873 passes Priestcroft Junction, 668 yards east of Boosbeck, in summer 1953. The line on the left is the Priestcroft Loop which drops down past North Skelton mine to North Skelton Junction where it joins the Saltburn-Crag Hall line. *J.W. Armstrong Trust*

The 1960 Sectional Appendix showed the Priestcroft Loop as a 2m 398yd 20mph through siding with an additional standage siding which could be entered at each end. Both lines were controlled by the signalmen at Priestcroft and North Skelton junctions. The through siding could be used as a through line in either direction under Absolute Block working by trains not carrying passengers. Passenger trains needing to use the through siding had to be accompanied by a pilotman in accordance with regulations for single line working by Train Staff & Ticket.

Left: Tiny Longacres signal cabin between North Skelton and Saltburn which controlled connections for Longacres mine on the east side of the line. The mine closed in the 1950s and, as can be seen, the box has attracted the attentions of vandals. *D. Simpson*

A bell, operated by bell-push in the weigh cabin adjacent to **North Skelton mine** road crossing has been affixed to signal post of No.9 mine outlet signal. Drivers of trains...which have to propel into the mine sidings must bring the train to a stand when the engine is completely... on the mine side of No. 9 signal. After the train has come to a stand, the guard must....close and secure the crossing gates against road traffic......then obtain permission from mine staff at the weigh cabin for the train to enter the mine. Having obtained...permission, the guard must operate the bell. When the driver hears the bell....he may commence propelling into the mine over the road crossing.
N.E. Region Sectional Appendix 1960.

Above: A J27 0-6-0 passes North Skelton Junction as it climbs up from Saltburn West with a class H goods for Skinningrove during the 1960s. The Priestcroft Loop has been singled at this point while the signal box looks the worse for subsidence. Heavy trains climbing the 1 in 70/72 from Saltburn West to Brotton sometimes needed assitance and it was common practice for the engine of a preceeding train to return to Upleatham or Redcar and bank the following train in the rear. Banking of trains conveying timber, castings or loads on two or more bolster wagons was not permitted. *Both pictures on this page by T.E. Rounthwaite.*

Below: North Skelton Junction looking south with the Priestcroft Loop curving away right towards North Skelton mine, Cleveland's last iron mine until it too closed in 1964. J27 0-6-0 No. 65788 leads iron ore from the Brotton direction towards Teesside along a line still carrying steel and potash trains in 2007.

Above: The headgear and spoil heap of Dorman Long's Kilton Mine stand tall as J26 0-6-0 No. 65762 pulls its load of ironstone away from the pit and approaches Lingdale Junction on 21st May 1959. The branch from Lingdale Mine(Pease & Partners until taken over by Dorman Long in 1952) comes in from the right while between the two a shallow cutting can just be made out. This was to have been the Cleveland Extension Mineral Railway to Glaisdale which was never completed. The Lingdale branch closed in February 1962 and the Kilton branch in February 1963. *Ken Hoole/Neville Stead collection*

The Kilton Mine branch was just over a mile long from the Brotton-Guisborough line at Kiltonthorpe Junction, and the Lingdale Mine branch 1 mile 184yds from Lingdale Jn. Both were worked according to One Engine in Steam regulations with a maximum line speed of 20mph.

Below: Brotton station looking west in the 1950s with the Saltburn line going right and the Guisborough line to the left. The 1956 Stations Handbook shows Brotton as having a 5-ton yard crane and able to handle general goods and livestock. The station closed to passengers when the Loftus service was axed on 2nd May 1960 and to goods in April 1967 but the yard received domestic coal until around1980. *J.W.Armstrong*

Above: With Skinningrove ironworks over in the left distance, Q6 0-8-0 No. 63430 pulls past Crag Hall signal box in 1958 with empty coke wagons for Newport yard. *J.W. Armstrong Trust*

Until the 1960s, the 6 miles 1324yds of double track from here to Saltburn West was controlled by Absolute Block signalling but by 1969 traffic had declined so much that it had been reduced to a single track goods line with a 30mph line speed worked by Staff & Ticket, the signal boxes at North Skelton and Brotton having closed. Further downgrading appeared in a May 1970 supplement to the Sectional Appendix showing the closure of Crag Hall box and the line operated by One Train Working regulations with no Staff, signals being electrically controlled to prevent more than one train being on the branch at a time. Crag Hall box was reopened in 1974 when the line was upgraded for the potash traffic. In 2007 the only track left here is a crossing loop and a single line into Skinningrove steelworks, but there are still semaphore signals.

Below: Most potash trains from Boulby are local workings to the Cleveland Potash wharf at Tees Dock or to Middlesbrough goods yard but on 6th May 1982 a long-haul of containerised potash to ICI's Severnside fertilizer plant in Bristol was launched. The Bellcode Books proprietor was closely involved with the launch and during a wild fit of imagination coined the 'Severn Sider' name for the train. On the launch day, English Electric Type 3 No. 37193 and Brush Type 2 No. 31332 draw the 'Severn Sider' past the steelworks. *S. Chapman*

Two views of Carlin How engine shed in the early 1950s.

The shed was built in the 1860s and later fitted with a timber extension. It closed in 1902 upon closure of Liverton mines but reopened in 1907. It closed again in 1921 and was demolished during the 1950s.

Top: The south end of the original brick shed with the timber extension at the far end.

Centre: The extension at the north end of the shed. Among locomotives allocated here by the NER were 0-6-0s for local mineral workings and the four 1037 class 0-6-0Ts, Nos. 1037, 1292/3/4 which were specially built in 1876 for the Skinningrove zig-zag where they worked for about 35 years.

Bottom: Loco facilities in the area included a turntable at Carlin How, seen here graced by WD 2-8-0 No. 90435 after working up from Newport on 4th June 1960.

All N.E. Stead collection

Above: Among the industrial gems employed by the Skinningrove Iron Works was *Minnie*, an 0-6-0ST built by Fox Walker & Co. of Bristol, works No. 358. She still looked spritely when caught flitting through the works sidings in the early 1950s despite being built as long ago as 1878 and even went on to receive an overhaul in 1960. Before going to Skinningrove, *Minnie* worked for Paddy Waddell on construction of the Cleveland Extension Mineral Railway and probably the Whitby-Loftus line as well. *Neville Stead collection*

Below: This strange contraption was even older. It was a vertical-boilered 0-4-0 tank engine built by Cochranes of Cargo Fleet in 1871 and worked on the jetty attached to the ironworks. The track is clearly dual gauge and probably carried a travelling crane. The jetty lines were linked to the clifftop works by an incline which can be seen reaching up to the blast furnace above the train. *Neville Stead collection*

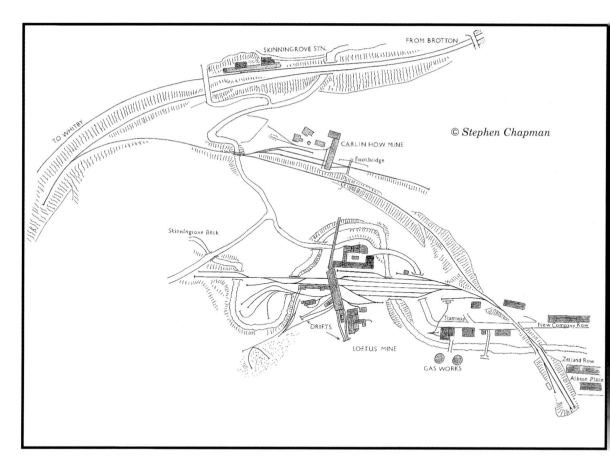

© Stephen Chapman

Above: The Skinningrove Zig-Zag as it was in 1914, just after Kilton Viaduct had been converted to an embankment and the first reversal relocated. Loftus mine closed in 1958 and the zig-zag with it.
The course of the railway is difficult to trace in 2007 but there is plenty to see of both Loftus and Carlin How mines and a footbridge still crosses the site of Carlin How mine sidings. *Not to scale*

Left This old postcard was copied by the railway company many years ago and ended up in the BR archive. It shows NER 1037 class 0-6-0T No. 1294 after coming to grief at the end the second reversal in the village centre some time in the very early 20th or late 19th century. The nearest row of houses is Albion Place and the large building in the centre of the picture the Miners' Institute.

Above: Loftus station(originally called Lofthouse) in the 1950s with A8 No. 69880 arriving on a Scarborough to Middlesbrough service. This was the end of the line following closure of the route to Whitby from 5th May 1958. Its remaining passenger service of three DMUs a day to and from Middlesbrough via Guisborough was axed on 2nd May 1960 and goods services withdrawn on 12th August 1963, after which the track was lifted back to Skinningrove steel works. A single line was reopened in 1974 to serve Boulby potash mine and in 2007 trains still pass by the station buildings. *Ken Hoole/Neville Stead collection*

Below: Loftus station layout as it was in 1914. *Not to scale*
The 1956 Handbook of Stations listed the goods yard as capable of dealing with all classes of freight traffic and equipped with a 5 ton crane. Other sidings listed in the area were: Carlin How public siding(general goods,) Carlin How engine shed, Skinningrove public coal depot, Skinningrove Ironworks, and the Scottish Agricultural Industries Ltd. basic slag works within the ironworks.

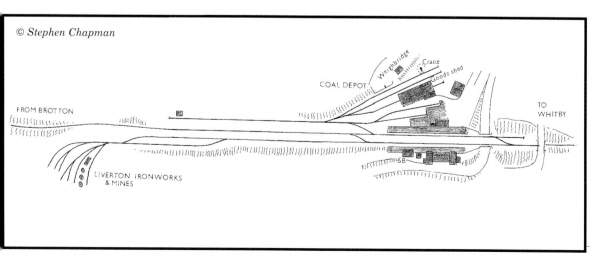

© Stephen Chapman

Above: The first station after Loftus on the line to Whitby was Grinkle, seen here looking north towards the tunnel in the early 1950s. Grinkle station (Easington until 1904) was temporarily closed to both passengers and goods in 1939, the closure being made permanent in 1955. In this view, the tiny signal box on the platform has also been switched out and boarded up with the signals permanently 'off' and the loop out of use. By 1957 the ramshackle building on the loop line's platform had been cleared away while the signal box had been gutted and was derelict but since 1974 this stretch of line has been alive with potash trains. *J.W. Armstrong Trust*

Below: The idyllic setting of this shot belies the fact that there were numerous mine workings in the area. L1 2-6-4T No. 67750 passes the village of Easington with a Whitby to Middlesbrough train in the mid-1950s. The space at each side of the single track suggests the previous existance of sidings here. *K. Hoole/N. Stead colln.*

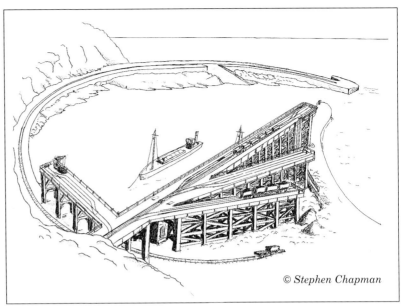

© Stephen Chapman

Above left: The long-since bricked up and overgrown exit from Palmers' ironstone mine in the cliff face at Port Mulgrave in July 1996 and, above right, how Port Mulgrave might have looked in its heyday.

A 'main and tail' rope-haulage system powered by a stationary steam engine pulled up to 800 tons of ore a day in 3ft gauge wagons out onto the long gantry where it was tipped into waiting barges. The two gantries to the right were for tipping ironstone onto the breakwater for storage when no vessels were present, and the one on the left for loading incoming coal which the line delivered to local communities. A steep incline hauled the ironstone back up from breakwater level to the main gantry. A 2ft gauge line ran round the breakwater for harbour maintenance.The mine eventually formed a mile-long tunnel, the inland end leading to a surface line worked by squat 0-4-0STs in Midland Red livery which ran to a mine situated in the valley of Easington Beck, not far from the main line at Boulby.

Below: L1 2-6-4T No. 67754 calls at Staithes with a Middlesbrough to Scarborough service in May 1958. The small signal box is on the right and on the left is one of the camping coaches which were also to be found at Sandsend and East Row. *A.L. Brown / Neville Stead collection*

Left: The rails are rusty and the gardens are becoming unkempt. This was Staithes station looking north towards the viaduct in August 1958, three months after closure. *Peter Cookson*

Staithes goods yard was equipped with a two ton crane but could only handle general goods. Considerable amounts of fish were once despatched.

Below: Two and three quarter miles south of Staithes, was Hinderwell(for Runswick Bay) station. This was it looking north on 7th October 1957 when the 11.40am Scarborough to Middlesbrough hauled by BR Standard Class 4 2-6-4T No. 80117 was calling. The small canopied goods shed is typical of those along this line. The goods yard here was better appointed than that at Staithes, also having a 2-ton crane but able to deal with all classes of freight. *J.F. Sedgewick/J.W. Armstrong Trust*

Above: Bulled-up L1 2-6-4T No. 67754 calls at Kettleness with a packed Whitby train on the 3rd May 1958, the last day of services. *I. Davidson / Colour-Rail BRE1616.*

Below: The Whitby, Redcar & Middlesbrough Union Railway was like many coastal lines in that it took on a completely different character during the few weeks of British summer. July would see it transformed from a meandering, lightly-used branch to something approaching main line status. In this view, the tank engines have given way to Ivatt Class 4 2-6-0 No. 43050 heading a five-coach Scarborough-Middlesbrough express over 63ft-high Sandsend Viaduct on 18th August 1955. *Ken Hoole / Neville Stead collection*

Above: Sandsend station looking towards the viaduct and Whitby on 18th August 1955. Sandsend was in fact the only station between Loftus and Whitby not to have a crossing loop. Although the goods yard was further south at East Row, Sandsend station also had a small yard with coal drops. It was also occupied by camping coaches while the 1956 Handbook of Stations listed it as just being able to handle general goods.

Below: As its name indicates, Sandsend is the northern extent of the beach from Whitby and a particularly fine beach it is at East Row where A5 4-6-2T No. 69838(51A) rumbles a Middlesbrough-bound train over the viaduct in 1955. A selection of period cars completes the scene which was changed for ever in 1960 when the viaduct, like all others on the line, was dismantled. Beyond the train is East Row goods shed and sidings which are occupied by two more camping coaches. The yard was listed as having a two ton crane but the freight it could handle was not specified. *Both Neville Stead collection*

Above: A scene which helps to explain why this line did not even last long enough to be closed by Beeching. Whitby shed's J25 0-6-0 No. 65663 travels empty handed as it crosses Newholme Beck Viaduct, south of Sandsend, in 1955 with only the guard's van forming the returning Whitby-Carlin How pick-up. Newholme Beck Viaduct reached a maximum height of 50ft and was 325ft long. *Ken Hoole/Neville Stead collection*

Below: Another lightweight train, the 4.20pm Middlesbrough to Scarborough hauled by BR Class 4MT 2-6-4T No. 80117 crosses Upgang Viaduct at 5.50pm on 31st May 1956. *David Holmes*
Most Middlesbrough-Whitby-Scarborough passenger trains were worked by Fairburn and BR Standard 2-6-4Ts from the start of the winter 1955/56 timetable and goods trains by BR Standard Class 3 2-6-0s. Brighton-built 80117 was allocated new to Whitby along with 80116 in May 1955, 80118-80120 following by July with Fairburn tank 42083 transferring there from Darlington in September.

Above: The south end of West Cliff station where BR 2-6-4T No. 80118 stands with a 1950s two-coach train. The goods yard, just visible beyond the train at the north end, was listed at the time as capable of handling only general goods, livestock, horse boxes and prize cattle vans and there was no crane. A private siding served the Urban District Council storeyard. *E.E. Smith / Neville Stead collection*

Below: Whitby West Cliff station in May 1958 with L1 2-6-4T No. 67764 waiting to leave for Middlesbrough. *J.C.W. Halliday / Colour-Rail BRE877*
Although out on a limb, West Cliff saw 32 timetabled Monday-Friday departures in high summer 1955, consisting of eight to Middlesbrough via Guisborough, two to Middlesbrough via Redcar, 10 to Scarborough and 12 to Whitby Town. Peak summer Saturdays saw another seven departures.

SHORT MEMORIES

The 1960 Sectional Appendix stated that passenger trains may be propelled from Bog Hall to West Cliff provided they consisted of no more than two coaches, that the brake compartment must be leading in which the guard must ride and have access to the automatic brake, and the speed must not exceed 10mph. When a class B train was propelled in accordance with these instructions, the headlamp could remain at the foot of the chimney with a tail lamp on the buffer beam.

Above: Whitby West Cliff closed to both passengers and goods on 12th June 1961 but the station stayed almost as it had been left that day for decades afterwards. This was the frontage of the main buildings in July 1996. On the platform side, even the canopy remained intact. *Stephen Chapman*

Below: In August 1955, BR Standard Class 3MT 2-6-0 No. 77013(51A) between West Cliff and Prospect Hill with what seems to be the 8am Darlington-Scarborough. *Peter Cookson*

91

Above: A8 No. 69885, allocated to 50E Scarborough, tackles the 1 in 54 from Whitby Town to West Cliff on a mid-1950s summer morning. *Peter Cookson*
The single line from Prospect Hill to Bog Hall was 1,485 yards long and was signalled by Electric Token. The line speed was 20mph.

Below: Having just passed beneath Larpool Viaduct, L1 2-6-4T No. 67765 descends towards Bog Hall Junction and Whitby Town with a train from West Cliff on 21st June 1957. This section of line and that over the viaduct was closed on 8th March 1965 when the Whitby-Scarborough service was withdrawn but was retained, disused, until 1973 pending potash traffic which failed to materialise. The brick viaduct stands 120ft high and 915ft long. It is still there and since 2000 has carried a footpath and cycle track. *Ken Hoole/Neville Stead collection*

Above: Whitby Town as we shall never see it again. The signal is off for the Metro-Cammell diesel multiple unit about to leave what is today the one remaining platform, L1 No. 67754 awaits its departure as BR Class 3 2-6-0 No. 77012 stands in the siding with a fish van and parcels stock. All this was stripped away in the 1980s and today only one train at a time can be seen here. The station became unstaffed in 1988 when parcels facilities were withdrawn. *A.L Brown / Neville Stead collection*

WHITBY-BATTERSBY-PICTON

Below: Ready to leave Whitby Town for Middlesbrough in 1957 is A8 No. 69852. Being 1930s rebuilds of North Eastern 4-4-4Ts, the A8s were the staple power on Cleveland passenger services for 25 years.
The steel girder awnings date from the early 1950s when they replaced the York & North Midland overall roof.
Ken Hoole / Neville Stead collection

D49/1 4-4-0 No. 62731 *Selkirkshire* prepares for departure with a Railway Correspondence & Travel Society railtour on 23rd June 1957. This engine was transferred from York to Selby shed that month. The signal box was made tall enough for the signalman to see over the goods shed next to it. *Neville Stead collection*

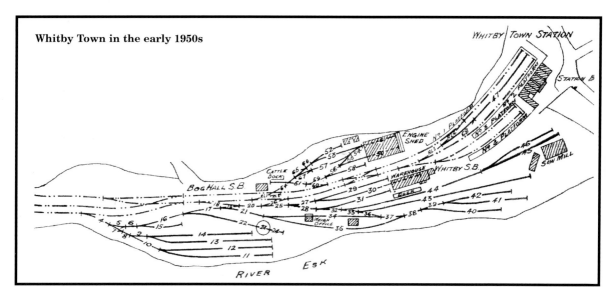

Whitby Town in the early 1950s

Locomotives allocated to 50G Whitby, January 1958

Fairburn Class 4 2-6-4T: 42083; J25 0-6-0: 65648; A8 4-6-2T: 69864/5; BR Standard Class 3 2-6-0: 77012/13; BR Standard Class 4 2-6-4T: 80116-20. Total: 11

Whitby engine shed, coded 50G in BR's York District, provided mainly locomotives to work the passenger services that radiated south, north and west from the busy fishing port and, consequently, closed on 6th April 1959 as services from the Malton direction were turned over to diesels. The shed was still standing in 2007, having been used as a chandler's store.

The 1950s scene above shows, from left, wagons of loco coal on the elevated track to the coal stage, the coaling crane, the engine shed, various A8 4-6-2Ts including 69864 nearest the camera, a G5 0-4-4T behind it and, beyond that a J27 0-6-0. Across the main lines on the right are the goods sidings, then the River Esk and up on the hill, Whitby Abbey, the inspiration behind Bram Stoker's Dracula. *Neville Stead collection*

Below: A scene illustrating the phenomenal amount of local goods traffic still reaching Whitby in the 1950s. Amid the wagons on an August evening in 1955, G5 0-4-4T No. 67240 is on coaching stock while J25 No. 65685 and Standard 4MT 2-6-4T No. 80119 are on shed. *Peter Cookson*

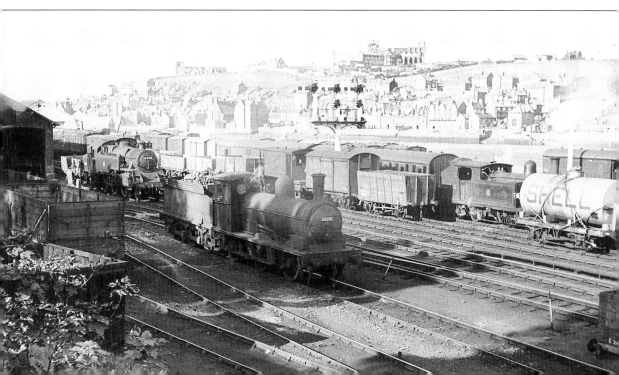

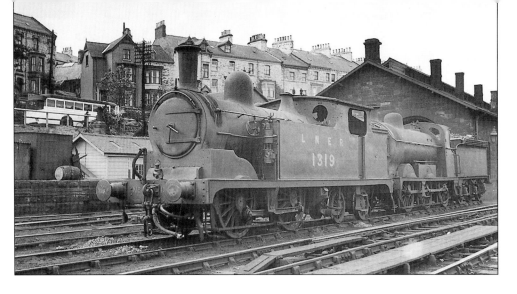

Left: A pre-nationalisation view with a G5 0-4-4T carrying the pre-1946 LNER number 1319 accompanied by an ex-Hull & Barnsley Railway J23 0-6-0. *Neville Stead collection*

Right: Whitby engine shed fully intact in July 1996, as it is in 2007. The different building style at the far (station) end shows that the 1847-built shed had been extended.

Below: The once common-place thrill of watching a big steam locomotive being turned can only be enjoyed at a handful of preserved railways and museums nowadays. Here Scarborough A8 No. 69879 is manually turned ready for working back home. *Neville Stead collection*

Above: A8 No. 69861 gets into its stride past Bog Hall signal box with the 6.10pm Whitby to Malton during August 1958. *Peter Cookson*

Below: V3 2-6-2T No. 67686 rolls past the recently renovated turntable and into Whitby at the head of a train from Middlesbrough conveying a horse box next to the engine. *Peter Cookson*

Above: The first station out of Whitby on the former Whitby & Pickering Railway, and the first of many River Esk crossings, is at Ruswarp. Here, B1 4-6-0 No. 61154 from Sheffield Darnall heads over the river with a York-bound stopping train. On the right, a bus can be seen held at the level crossing after just having crossed the bow girder road bridge while Larpool Viaduct forms the distant horizon. *Ken Hoole/N. Stead collection*

Below: Sleights station looking towards Whitby in August 1958. In high summer 1957, this station was served by 14 Monday-Friday trains to Whitby(including through carriages from King's Cross at 5.19pm on Fridays,) five to Middlesbrough via Battersby, one to Battersby, four to Malton, two to Goathland and the 7.7pm to York(plus an extra Friday morning train to York.) The through carriages from London also ran on Saturdays, as did a through train to Leeds at 2.19pm and two to York. In summer 2006 there were just four weekday trains to Whitby and four to Middlesbrough but at least the station remains open. Nowadays, the track is single, serving the right hand platform though the buildings survive almost outwardly unchanged. The signal box is closed and boarded up while a stop board has replaced the starting signal. *Peter Cookson*

Above: On the same occasion as the previous picture, A8 No. 69861 rolls into Sleights with the 4pm Malton to Whitby complete with the customary fish van returning for another load of Whitby cod. The large throng of passengers have been on a guided walk from Whitby. *Peter Cookson*

Below: On the approach from Sleights, Q6 0-8-0 No. 63374 waits for the road into Grosmont with the returning Thornaby trip 94, the Newport-Whitby pick-up. The picture does not have a precise date, but if it is a Monday, Wednesday or Friday, 63374's next move will be to shunt at Grosmont if required. *Neville Stead collection*

SHORT MEMORIES

May 1964: Clayton Type 1 diesels D8589/90 allocated to Thornaby. D8591 follows in July.

1.10.64: A4 Pacific 60002 arrives at Cochrane's, Cargo Fleet, for cutting up.

24.4.65: D1576 takes a football special from Whitby to King's Cross for the FA Amateur Cup Final, assisted by D399 as far as Battersby.

Summer 1965: Whitby reports 18,461 visitors compared with 51,691 in 1964, before the Malton & Scarborough lines closed.

Left: The layout at Grosmont as it was in 1942.

Diagram labels: AGREEMENT 3 MARCH 1899 · HODGSMAN'S SLAG CRUSHING WORKS · DARLINGTON DISTRICT (D.E.) · YORK DISTRICT (D.E.) · BRIDGE Nº 94 · NORTH YORKSHIRE & CLEVELAND BR. · HODGSMAN'S SLAG CRUSHING WORKS · CROSMONT SIGNAL BOX · GROSMONT JUNCTION · FROM WHITBY · GROSMONT STATION · LOADING DOCK 67 YDS. · PLATFORM 84 YDS. · PLATFORM 81 YDS. · BRIDGE Nº 42 · Nº 41 · TO PICKERING · BRIDGE Nº 43

Below: Grosmont at 12.3pm on 16th April 1958 and J27 0-6-0 No. 65848 takes the Pickering line with the returning Malton-Whitby pick-up. This train might well have shunted Woodland's Siding, on the north side of the line about a mile and a half east of Grosmont where some track remained, disconnected from the running line, in early 2007. With J27 No. 65894 based at the North Yorkshire Moors Railway, a scene like this could theoretically be recreated today. The brickworks chimney is long gone but some old kilns are still there to see in 2007. *David Holmes*

The 1960 BR North Eastern Region Sectional Appendix shows the Battersby-Grosmont line as worked by Electric Token with signal boxes at Battersby, Castleton (7 miles 576yds from Battersby,) Glaisdale (5miles 1150yds from Castleton,) and Grosmont (3m 269yds.) There was a crossing loop holding 32 wagons, engine & brake van at Castleton along with an Up refuge siding holding 37 wagons, engine & van, a Down refuge siding at Danby holding 48 wagons, engine & van, and a crossing loop at Glaisdale holding 48 wagons, engine & van. Maximum line speed was 45mph. The loops at Castleton and Glaisdale.were the only additional lines shown in the 1969 Sectional Appendix.

Above: Most stations between Grosmont and Battersby have kept their original character, largely because their buildings have been retained in private use. The main changes are the removal of sidings, crossing loops where these have existed and signalling. This was Egton looking west, on 2nd September 1997. The goods yard here was listed as able to handle only general goods and livestock besides having the customary(stone-built) coal drops and it closed on 2nd August 1965. *Stephen Chapman*

Below: Half a mile east of Glaisdale is this bridge over the Esk, seen with G5 0-4-4T No. 67343 crossing at the head of a Stockton to Whitby service in August 1953. The original stone bridge was swept away by floodwater in 1930 and the line was severed for 10 months while a new single span girder bridge was built to replace it. Three months after it was completed another flood swept the new span into the river after the water scoured a new course behind one of the abutments. Again, the line was severed for 11 months while the span was recovered and incorporated in the present two-span replacement completed in 1932. *J.W. Armstrong Trust*

Above: Glaisdale station, looking towards Battersby, in May 1982 with Brush Type 2 No. 31153 on the Tees Yard-Whitby pick-up. The station had seen few changes since the small goods yard closed on 2nd August 1965. Even in 2007 it looks remarkably similar, except that the semaphore signals have given way to automatic searchlight signals and the signal box is closed and boarded up. *Malcolm Roughley*

Below: Two miles west of Glaisdale comes Lealholm with its platform signal box, as seen here from a Whitby-bound train in the 1950s when there was a crossing loop and two platforms. The goods depot here possessed a one-ton crane and was able to handle general goods, livestock, horse boxes and prize cattle vans but closed on 2nd August 1965. There was another siding at Houlsyke, between here and Danby. *J.W. Armstrong Trust*

Private sidings between Grosmont and Battersby listed in the 1956 Handbook of Stations were:
Grosmont: Balcony Slag Works; Eldon Brick Co., Hodsman & Sons slag crushing works.
Glaisdale: Thos. Roberts (Westminster) Ltd.
Castleton: General Refractories Ltd. Ganister Works.
Commondale: Commondale Brick & Pipe Co.
The 1969 Sectional Appendix stated that traffic into and out of Tunnicliffe Siding, between Castleton and Battersby, must always be worked by trains travelling in the Up direction because of the gradient.

Above: The Esk Valley line was rudely awoken on 2nd August 1981 when top link express power of the highest order traversed its meandering metals. The 99-ton 3,300bhp Deltic No. 55002 *The King's Own Yorkshire Light Infantry* is seen passing through Danby with a railtour to Whitby. More used to eating East Coast main line miles at 100mph, the Deltic would have to settle for a much more sedate speed on this line. The milepost states that Danby is 21 miles from Picton. The goods yard which could deal only with general goods, livestock, horse boxes and prize cattle vans until closing on 2nd August 1965, was behind the station building. *Neville Stead*

Below: The unstaffed halt at Commondale in August 1967 with its tiny building and sleeper platform. The Brick & Pipe Co.'s line went off to the right beyond the station and in 2007 the abutments of a bridge taking it over the river complete with some rails are still visible from passing trains. *Neville Stead collection*

Above: With its crossing loop, two platforms, signal box and siding, Castleton Moor retained an air of importance into the 1980s and was the next passing point after Glaisdale. This is how it still looked on 2nd August 1981 when Deltic No. 55002 *The King's Own Yorkshire Light Infantry* crossed a Middlesbrough-Whitby Metro-Cammell Class 101 DMU while returning its railtour to Middlesbrough. The loop and Castleton box were abolished in 1982 and the station reduced to a one-platform halt. The 1956 Handbook of Stations listed Castleton as having a 5 ton crane and the ability to handle every class of freight. *Neville Stead*

Between Castleton and Grosmont, bridges (though not earthworks) were built for double track.

The 1950s saw some rationalisation on the Esk Valley line and peaceful Kildale lost its crossing loop, signal box, station staff and goods yard in June 1956 when it was reduced to a one platform halt.

This is how it looked before that with A8 No. 69861 on a Middlesbrough-Whitby train. *J.W. Armstrong Trust*

104

Above: Battersby station throat in 1989 was still a delightful reminder of the classic railway, and had hardly changed since the 1950s. Within a few years the whole lot had been banished to history when the signal box and its semaphores were replaced by the line's revolutionary 'no signalman token' signalling system under the overall supervision of Nunthorpe box. Battersby became an automated junction and crossing place, and one of the line's three remote token stations, the token lockers containing traditional instruments. Two-aspect colour light signals now control movements here, the track to the bay platform has gone and a ground frame operates points for the run-round siding. *Stephen Chapman*

Below: Originally called Ingleby Junction, Battersby station has always existed mainly for railway operational purposes. This is the station looking east in August 1967, the milepost showing it to be 12 miles from Picton. There was once a NER pattern footbridge connecting the two platforms and a long-reach water crane between the house and low building on the right. *Neville Stead collection*

By 1960, the single line from Battersby to Nunthorpe East was one section worked by Electric Token. The signal box at Great Ayton had been abolished but non-passenger trains could be "locked in" at the sidings there so that other trains could pass. The 1960 Sectional Appendix contained a full page instruction regarding this operation. It began: "An Intermediate Token instrument is provided near the platform at Great Ayton station for use when it is necessary to shunt a train not conveying passengers clear of the running line for passing other trains. Three ground frames are also provided, one situated at the crossover opposite the platform, one at the goods yard connection, and the third at the mines siding connection. The signalman at Nunthorpe East or Battersby must instruct the guard as to whether the train has to be locked in at Great Ayton....There then followed instructions to guards on use of the ground frames and the procedure to be followed when locking a train in.

Within a mile and a half at Great Ayton were five connections with industrial railways probing upwards into the hillsides to reach iron and whinstone mines and quarries.

Approaching from Nunthorpe, on the west side of the line about a mile and a quarter before Great Ayton, were Bradley's Langbaurgh whinstone quarry sidings. Stone was brought from the quarries on a 2ft gauge line worked by an 0-4-0T, *Clara*, built by S. Lewin of Poole, Dorset. It was abandoned in the 1930s but the standard gauge sidings remained in use for some time afterwards.

Immediately after passing under the Guisborough-Great Ayton road, was a spur going south east to a narrow gauge system which began with a steep incline to reach Roseberry ironstone mines 750ft up on the south east edge of Roseberry Topping. From the incline top, the railways were once worked by a Black Hawthorn 0-4-0ST *Roseberry* but after about 1910 a 'tail and main' haulage system powered by a stationary steam engine was used. At its peak, the Roseberry system sent 1000 tons of ore a day to the Tees Furnace Co.'s Lackenby and Skinningrove works but it closed in 1924.

After another road overbridge came a north-facing connection with Winn's whinstone quarry situated on Cliff Ridge. The narrow gauge internal lines here, which ceased operation around 1918, also had a Lewin 0-4-0T.

Until 1926 a fascinating 1.25-mile 2ft 3.5in. gauge line to Gribdale whinstone mines left the east side of Great Ayton station and followed the Gribdale Valley before climbing 300ft to the mines via a reversal and a curve around north-facing Ayton Bank. This system was also worked by a Black Hawthorn 0-4-0ST called *Roseberry*. An overhead cableway carried ironstone down to Winn's sidings.

Finally, about 200 yards south of the station a south easterly connection led to a double track incline(possibly narrow gauge) which ascended 450ft to Pease's iron mine in the north face of Coate Moor. It closed in 1928.

By 1956, just the connection to Cliff Rigg siding remained but in 2007 many traces of these systems can easily be seen from passing trains. For example, a shallow embankment marks the route of Bradley's narrow gauge line. *Information from a detailed account by T.E. Rounthwaite in The Railway Observer, May 1962.*

Left: Battersby's three-road engine shed situated on the south side of the station, was built to provide power for the Rosedale iron ore trains. First built in 1877, replaced by this one in 1889 and closed in 1895, it was not demolished until the mid-1960s. After closure it was used as a first world war store for dining cars. The track was removed in the 1920s and it spent some time as a rifle range. It is seen here isolated from the railway on 1st October 1963. *K. Hoole/N. Stead colln.*

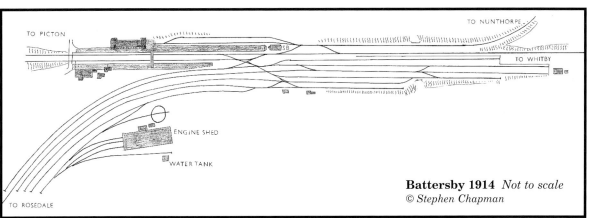

Battersby 1914 *Not to scale*
© *Stephen Chapman*

SHORT MEMORIES

Spring 1966: Most remaining steam workings to Tees Yard, South Bank and Skinningrove now covered by West Hartlepool engines.

Sept. 1967: All steam working ends upon the closure of West Hartlepool and Sunderland sheds.

4.4.69: Trains of 3x100 ton torpedo wagons start carrying molten iron from Cargo Fleet to Consett.

Above: The view from Battersby station looking towards Stokesley and Picton with Brush Type 2 No. 31153 just having run round its train, the Whitby goods, in May 1982. The line beyond here closed in 1965 and since then the only bit of it remaining has been the run round loop shown in the picture. *Malcolm Roughley*

Above: The Rosedale railway and the iron mines passed into history before the era covered by the Railway Memories series but they were such a key part of the Cleveland railway scene that mention has to be made for the sake of completeness. This late 19th century postcard of what looks like East Rosedale shows mine tubs in the foreground and main line wagons being loaded on the lower level.
Stephen Chapman archive

Left: Ingleby station, serving the village of Ingleby Greenhow, was just three quarters of a mile west of Battersby but while Battersby lives on, Ingleby closed to both passengers and goods on 14th June 1954. Here, G5 0-4-4T No. 67288 restarts a Stockton train, possibly the 5.50pm from Whitby.

As the line from here onwards was by this time worked as a single line, 67288 will have to draw its train forward and then set back onto the Down (eastbound) road for the remainder of its journey to Picton. *Neville Stead collection.*

Above: Stokesley was the most important intermediate station between Battersby and Picton, serving as it did a small market town. It too closed to passengers on 14th June 1954 but remained open for parcels. When through goods traffic ended in December 1958 it became the end of the line from Battersby. The goods yard, listed in 1956 as having a 1.5 ton crane and capable of dealing with all kinds of freight, stayed in business until 2nd August 1965. With closure to passengers less than a month away, G5 0-4-4T No. 67343 of 51C West Hartlepool enters the station with a Whitby train in May 1954. *J.W. Armstrong Trust*

Below: Stokesley station viewed from the west with G5 No. 67240(50G) on the eastbound line with a Whitby to Stockton train in May 1954.
The 1960 Sectional Appendix showed the surviving 3 mile 1349yd line from Stokesley to Battersby as worked according to One Engine in Steam regulations with a maximum line speed of 20mph. *J.W. Armstrong Trust*

Above: Three miles west of Stokesley was Sexhow, seen here with Whitby A8 No. 69858 at the head of a Stockton train. In the distance, wagons can be seen stored on the Up line.The 1956 Stations Handbook listed this station as having a goods yard equipped with a 2 ton crane and capable of dealing with general goods, livestock, horse boxes and prize cattle vans while the station was still open for parcels. Sexhow closed completely on 1st December 1958 along with the Stokesley-Picton section of the line. *J.W. Armstrong Trust*

Left: Potto was next along the line, just a mile and a quarter west of Sexhow. Cyclists wait patiently as G5 No. 67343 slowly moves its Whitby to Stockton train out of the platform.

J.W. Armstrong Trust

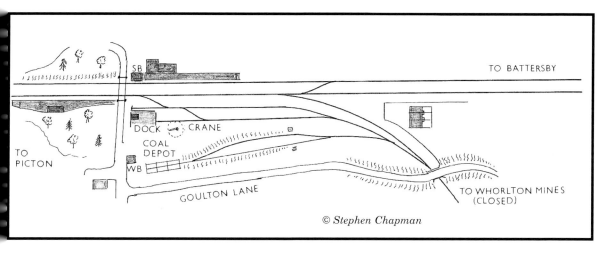

© *Stephen Chapman*

Above: The layout at Potto as it was in 1913. *Not to scale*

Potto station also remained open for parcels after closure to passengers on 14th June 1954 while the goods yard was listed in 1956 as equipped with a 5 ton crane and able to handle general goods, livestock, horse boxes and prize cattle vans, and carriages and motor cars by passenger or parcels train.

Below: Between Potto and Picton, the line crossed the A19 road at Trenholme Bar where in the early 1950s a manually operated gated level crossing was still adequate for both road and rail traffic. Here, J27 0-6-0 No. 65861 from York shed enters the station with the returning Whitby-Eaglescliffe pick-up. Once again, Trenholme Bar remained open for parcels after the end of passenger services while the goods yard was listed as able to handle all types of freight though it had no permanent crane. *J.W. Armstrong Trust*

In the 19th Century this line carried ironstone trains from Whorlton and Rosedale to Ferryhill in County Durham .

Above: G5 No. 67345 crosses the A19 as it leaves Trenholme Bar with what appears to be the 5.50pm Whitby to Stockton. After closure in December 1958, the section from here to Picton was used for storing surplus wagons. Eventual widening of the A19 has virtually obliterated the station. *J.W. Armstrong Trust*

Below: The fireman of G5 No. 67343 hands the single line staff to the signalman at Picton as his train from Whitby leaves the North Yorkshire & Cleveland branch and joins the Leeds-Newcastle Leeds Northern main line for the remainder of its journey to Stockton. *J.W. Armstrong Trust*